Childhood and society

ISSUES IN SOCIETY

Series Editor: Tim May

Childhood and society
Growing up in an age
of uncertainty

NICK LEE

OPEN UNIVERSITY PRESS
Buckingham • Philadelphia

Open University Press
Celtic Court
22 Ballmoor
Buckingham
MK18 1XW

email: enquiries@openup.co.uk
world wide web: www.openup.co.uk

and
325 Chestnut Street
Philadelphia, PA 19106, USA

First Published 2001

A catalogue record of this book is available from the British Library

ISBN 0 335 20608 5 (pb)   0 335 20609 3 (hb)

Library of Congress Cataloging-in-Publication Data
Lee, Nick, 1968–
    Childhood and society : growing up in an age of uncertainty / Nick Lee.
        p.   cm. — (Issues in society)
    Includes bibliographical references and index.
    ISBN 0–335–20609–3 — ISBN 0–335–20608–5 (pbk.)
    1. Sozialization. 2. Children. 3. Child development. I. Title. II. Series.

HQ783.L4 2001
305.23—dc21   2001021071

Typeset by Graphicraft Limited, Hong Kong
Printed in Great Britain by Biddles Limited, Guildford and Kings Lynn

To Mum and Dad with love

Contents

Series editor's foreword

Collectively, the social sciences contribute to a greater understanding of the dynamics of social life, as well as explanations for the workings of societies in general. Yet they are often not given due credit for this role and much writing has been devoted to why this should be the case. At the same time, we are living in an age in which the role of science in society is being re-evaluated. This has led to both a defence of science as the disinterested pursuit of knowledge and an attack on science as nothing more than an institutionalized assertion of faith, with no greater claim to validity than mythology and folklore. These debates tend to generate more heat than light.

In the meantime, the social sciences, in order to remain vibrant and relevant, will reflect the changing nature of these public debates. In so doing they provide mirrors upon which we can gaze in order to understand not only what we have been and what we are now, but to inform possibilities about what we might become. This is not simply about understanding the reasons people give for their actions in terms of the contexts in which they act and analyzing the relations of cause and effect in the social, political and economic spheres, but also concerns the hopes, wishes and aspirations that people, in their different cultural ways, hold.

In any society that claims to have democratic aspirations, these hopes and wishes are not for the social scientist to prescribe. For this to happen it would mean that the social sciences were able to predict human behaviour with certainty. One theory and one method, applicable to all times and places, would be required for this purpose. The physical sciences do not live up to such stringent criteria, whilst the conditions in societies which provided for this outcome, were it even possible, would be intolerable. Why? Because a necessary condition of human freedom is the ability to have acted otherwise and thus to imagine and practice different ways of organizing societies and living together.

It does not follow from the above that social scientists do not have a valued role to play, as is often assumed in ideological attacks upon their place and function within society. After all, in focusing upon what we have been and what we are now, what we might become is inevitably illuminated: the retrospective and prospective become fused. Therefore, whilst it may not the province of the social scientist to predict our futures, they are, given not only their understandings and explanations, but equal positions as citizens, entitled to engage in public debates concerning future prospects.

This new international series was devised with this general ethos in mind. It seeks to offer students of the sciences, at all levels, a forum in which ideas and topics of interest are interrogated in terms of their importance for understanding key social issues. This is achieved through a connection between style, structure and content that aims to be both illuminating and challenging in terms of its evaluation of those issues, as well as representing an original contribution to the subject under discussion.

Given this underlying philosophy, the series contains books on topics that are driven by substantive interests. This is not simply a reactive endeavour in terms of reflecting dominant social and political preoccupations, it is also proactive in terms of an examination of issues which relate to and inform the dynamics of social life and the structures of society that are often not part of public discourse. Thus, what is distinctive about this series is an interrogation of the assumed characteristics of our current epoch in relation to its consequences for the organization of society and social life, as well as its appropriate mode of study.

Each contribution contains, for the purposes of general orientation, as opposed to rigid structure, three parts. First, an interrogation of the topic that is conducted in a manner that renders explicit core assumptions surrounding the issues and/or an examination of the consequences of historical trends for contemporary social practices. Second, a section which aims to 'bring alive' ideas and practices by considering the ways in which they directly inform the dynamics of social relations. A third section then moves on to make an original contribution to the topic. This encompasses possible future forms and content, likely directions for the study of the phenomena in question, or an original analysis of the topic itself. Of course, it might be a combination of all three.

The very idea of possibilities for the future organization of social relations is related to the potentials that are taken to exist in the present. What we were, what we are and what we might become are linked in various ways, but it does not follow that this is determining. However, the very categories we employ to make sense of stages in our life course can be both empowering and constraining. There is a particular stage which is more pertinent to the idea of potentiality than any other: childhood. The ways in which adults view children and how they govern their activities is given in their contemporary practices. The question, of course, is whether these serve to maximize their potential or seek to constrain it in the name of the dominant ideas of the present?

Within the British context the certainties of the adult world are manifest in government policies which inform processes and practices within schools. Here it may be argued that we are witnessing a slide from education to training. Education is about the power and freedom of thought including, where deemed necessary, the ability to think otherwise. Nevertheless, children are required to reproduce conventional wisdom which is tested at regular intervals from an early age. Inevitably, in using criteria they are then compared with others and this produces images of what they are and what potential they possess. Texts are constructed accordingly and claims are made concerning 'progress' and 'efficient' and 'effective' teaching practices. Children are not only compared, but also contrasted and what proud parent can afford to ignore such a process?

Nick Lee turns his attention to the issues that underlie such practices: for example, ideas of being and becoming and dependence and independence. As he notes in his preface, the idea of taking childhood seriously might appear, at first glance, odd. Yet if we are concerned with what we might become, taking childhood seriously is fundamental to this endeavour. However, whilst recognizing the legitimacy of this activity, children are often regarded as those who should be 'seen', but not 'heard'. Spaces and places are demarcated accordingly and those who do so and seek to police such boundaries are those who apparently have never been children and if such an admission is apparent they were 'different' from the current generation.

Such views are based upon the certainties that come with the maintenance of boundaries which, upon examination, are not rigid, but fluid. At one level the idea of an age of certainty regarding the differences between the realms of adult and childhood may be nothing more than expressions of nostalgia for that which did not exist. Now, however, there is generally believed to be more fluidity. Whilst experts are there to reassure those anxious about being a parent there is no manual or template which can prepare them for this new role and the advice itself is not static, but subject to continual change. Similarly, as economic globalization questions the independence of the state, so therefore is the idea of children being dependent upon the state itself open to question. As governments fall uncritically at the alter of consumer capitalism, alongside an increasing regulation of the school curriculum, ambiguities are bound to increase. Modes of consumption then emerge with children becoming the targets of advertisers as the technicians of persuasion. The reaction is a heightening of what has been termed 'pester power' and the lives of children, as with adults, are then opened up to alternative forms of seduction and regulation. Taking the implications of these changes means that new ways of understanding childhood are required. Childhood, understood as the process of becoming towards a mature state, can find itself in question. Differences between adults and children are often thought to require further socialization on the part of the latter in order that they conform to the expectations of the former. This undermines the validity of expressions of difference which are seen to be in need of 'repair' according to dominant modes of rationality.

Finding itself in question, different ideas of 'becoming' are now required when it comes to understanding childhood. It is to the expressions and reasons for this fluidity and its manifestations in various places – including city streets, home and school, forms of national and global regulation and testimony in courts – that Nick Lee turns his analytic attention. Children can be constituted as threats and this can prompt extraordinary acts of barbarism from the adult world. In Brazil this has been graphically illustrated in situations where off duty police officers have opened fire on groups of street children. Having murdered them, such acts are condoned on the basis that these children are not human, but instead more like animals who exhibit subhuman traits and so are a threat to social order.

These 'particular' children are taken to be the cause, not the symptom, of social and economic decline. Thus removed from the burden of the problems they have created, the adult world can target certain children as manifestations of problems that are taken to lie beyond their responsibility. The same underlying ideas, with obvious differences in consequence, can be found in approaches to inner city disorder in Britain. The turning of political issues into technocratic administrative solutions leads to a by-passing of matters of inequality to focus upon schemes such as curfew orders, parenting orders and so on. The result is the same: adult concerns with order are played out on poor children who are regarded as the source of social disorder.

The discussion and analysis in this book is highly illuminating. At the end of the book Nick Lee asks if the sociology of childhood must become like the 'mature' discipline itself? Following an account of issues associated with agency and convention, he turns to an 'ethics of motion'. This dynamic approach, he argues, can allow for positions to undertake research on children, but does not foreclose the possibilities that are evident in conventional approaches and so allows for 'extensions' to understanding and experience.

A process of 'becoming-adult' does not allow for creativity and imagination in play to be the sole preserve of children, thereby reproducing a romantic image of childhood. Instead it allows for an examination of the ranges of extension that are available at different stages in the life course and thus opens up the possibility for thinking differently not only about childhood, but also adulthood. The implications of this position are worthy of the same effort that goes into the maintenance of the boundaries between the supposed self-evidence of the two worlds. This book should be read, therefore, not only by social scientists, but all those concerned with what they are in terms of what they have been and thus might become.

Tim May

Preface and acknowledgements

I first became interested in 'growing up' through Rex Stainton Rogers' classes in social and developmental psychology at Reading University. Rex seemed to use teaching as an excuse to spread a generous and disorderly spirit among his students. He had Les Murray's (1991) 'quality of sprawl' in spades, a quality, never destructive or malicious, that assembles alternative orders on the hoof and cheerfully accepts human diversity and fallibility.

I worked for a while as a 'play-worker' for Reading Borough Council. At the time, the job of the play-worker was to establish a space for 5–11-year-old children that was quite unlike school. In play-work, adults were not primarily authority figures and were certainly not 'experts'. It was not our job to control children (beyond issues of physical safety and bullying) but, instead, to help them realize their imaginations in drawing, modelling, sports, games and stories. Doing this job made me think about dependence and independence. The children were often very keen to involve adult play-workers in settling arguments and organizing games. Did this mean that they needed a grown-up to validate their activities and opinions? Was it a sign of children's dependence? In some ways, it was. They knew that to be allowed to play in some places they had to be supervised. In another way it meant something quite different – adults were valuable as a resource, a 'hook' on which to hang a game. Of course it helped that we had privileged access to the toy-store.

I started the odd business of taking childhood seriously as a doctoral student. Here I was not so much concerned with children themselves as with what expert adults made of them. I followed police and social workers as they tried to implement new policies and practices for dealing with cases of suspected child abuse. I came to realize how dependent they were in doing this difficult work on 'extensions' like official forms, guidelines and even the structure of the buildings they worked in. Just like the children I had worked with, they had to have hooks to hang their activities on too.

This book is an attempt to supplement the social study of childhood. Existing sociologies of childhood are diverse in the research methods they use and the goals that they pursue, but the field has been drawn together throughout the 1990s by a common commitment to the recognition of children as 'beings' who have 'voices' that are worth listening to. It still astonishes me that any effort has been required to establish this. Part of the purpose of this book, then, is to explain just why this effort has been necessary, why it is that children and adults have ever been thought of as fundamentally different types of persons, why, in other words, we need the sociology of childhood.

For all its faults, the being/becoming division that I discuss throughout the book did at least allow for some very limited recognition of the diversity of human life. Like many other dichotomies, such as male/female, gay/ straight and black/white, however, it allowed for only two ways of being human and asserted one as standard and the other as deviant. When we 'multiply' becoming later in the book we shall be pointing out one way to allow for the recognition of the unlimited diversity of ways of becoming human. I like to think that Rex would have enjoyed this.

Many thanks to Tim May and Justin Vaughan for making the production of this book such a pleasant process.

I would also like to thank the following people for helping me to think: Rex and Wendy Stainton Rogers; Rolland Munro and Joanna Latimer; Alan Prout, Jo Moran-Ellis and Priscilla Alderson; Bob Cooper, Steve Brown and John Law; Emily Campbell; the students who have taken my 'constructions of childhood' course; and Arabella, Jamie, Albhi, Eliza and Saskia.

Introduction: childhood and human variation

Humans differ from one another in numerous ways. Variations in sex, shape, size and skin colour have formed the basis of social hierarchies in many different times and places. External appearances have often been taken to say something about people's intrinsic natures. In many circumstances, being one human variant rather than another has had serious consequences for people's life chances and the degree of respect and personal dignity that they have been allowed. Chronological age is among the axes of human variability that have been linked to the social distribution of dignity and respect. Children can be marked out as a social group, distinguished by the visibility of their low chronological age. Their points of view, opinions and desires have often been ignored because their age has been taken as a sign that they are not worth listening to.

Some commentators, feeling that this treatment is unjust, have sought to break the links that have been forged between external appearances and children's intrinsic natures. In this vein, it has been argued that variations in chronological age are not nearly so important in shaping childhoods as are the attributions that societies make about children on the basis of their external appearances. Childhood on this view is 'socially constructed'. One of the problems that this constructionist approach to childhood has faced is that it tends to interpret all differences between adults and children as works of imagination. Thus, when this approach meets people who think it is only right and proper that children's voices be muted, the only resource it has to convince them otherwise is to tell them that they are deluded.

The constructionist approach to childhood draws strength from a contemporary ethical view that all humans should be treated 'equally'. When translating this ethical view into theoretical and empirical study it is all too easy to try to confirm it by painting a picture of all humans, regardless of chronological age, as fundamentally the same. Awareness of human variation is sacrificed to remove the potential for unjust attributions. So the study of childhood involves a tension between recognizing human variation – which carries the risk of allowing unjust attributions to be made – and discounting human variation – which carries the risk of overemphasizing the ability of imagination to shape the world. These tensions around the facts of human variation form the intellectual context of the book.

In Part one we ask how it is that variation in chronological age has come to form the basis of social distributions of rights, responsibilities, dignity and respect in the contemporary world. Chapters 1 and 2 offer an account of how and why the category 'human' has, throughout modernity, been divided into adult 'human beings' and child 'human becomings'. Chapter 3 reports on attempts that are currently being made by sociologists of childhood to resist this common-sense division. Whatever differences there may be between adults and children, contemporary sociologies of childhood urge that children be treated equally, at least in terms of recognizing that children have views and perspectives of their own. On this view, all humans, regardless of chronological age, are and should be treated as 'beings'.

In Part one, we also paint a picture of the late-twentieth and early-twenty-first centuries as an 'age of uncertainty', arguing both that adulthood can no longer be understood as the state of stable completion and self-possession on which 'being-hood' once rested, and that childhood is increasingly open to ambiguity. The nature of adult 'being' is becoming unclear just as the question of children's status as either 'beings' or 'becomings' begins to look unanswerable. Building on this assessment of the contemporary condition of adulthood and childhood, Part two then examines a number of locations where the contemporary ambiguity of childhood is brought into sharp focus: the streets of the world's cities; the institutions of the family home and the school; and the national and global regulation of childhood. We argue that these ambiguities demand a novel response from childhood researchers – to withdraw from attempts to resolve childhood's ambiguity so that they can better study the social distribution and consequences of ambiguity.

Part three lays out the conceptual resources and research orientations that can help social studies of childhood become more sensitive to childhood ambiguity and less reliant on problematic notions of human 'being'. It offers a new way to understand and to chart human variation. We advance the view that there are no 'human beings' but that there are instead potentially unlimited numbers of ways of 'becoming human'. The emphasis of work based on this view is placed on detecting and understanding 'real stabilities' (Lee 1998a) in patterns of human becoming, rather than in detecting and criticizing sets of attributions about people made on the basis of their chronological age. Part three then is an attempt to turn our attention away from arguments over whether or not visible age differences should be taken as a sign of intrinsic difference, as a reliable or unreliable basis for attributions, and toward variations in ways that people are 'extended' (Munro 1996) by other people, the material world and technological devices.

The aim is to give a positive alternative to age-based discrimination by maximizing our acknowledgement of human variation and by showing that there are many ways to 'become human', some more and some less available to children.

The new direction that we lay out for the social study of childhood (and by implication the study of all human becoming) comes in the form of a call for an 'immature' sociology. To call for immaturity is not to suggest that researchers should try to 'see the world as children see it'. Instead it is to advance the view that sociologists of childhood should seek confidence and inspiration in the creative potential that comes with working in their relatively new field of social study, rather than seek to model their work on the problem space defined by 'mainstream' sociology. It is, in other words, a call for the imagination and creativity needed to understand and to intervene in a world that is increasingly revealing itself as 'unfinished', a world in which mediascapes and short-term flexibilities of planning allow the imaginations of the powerful to be realized perhaps too rapidly. Thus the chapters in Part three may be read as an attempt to understand the relative speeds of change and modes of interaction of the imagination, the materials (bodily and inorganic) and the institutions that together comprise the social world. It is out of this vision of social inquiry that our redescription of 'growing-up' as 'slowing-down' evolved.

Finally, a word on definitions. Given that chronological age has been so important to the definition of childhood, I should give some indication of what ages I take 'childhood' to refer to. On one legalistic view, childhood extends from year zero to 18. A few of the issues under discussion here are relevant to the higher end of that range, but the bulk of the argument concerns children in the middle years. I have not explicitly excluded the very young, but I do feel that the patterns of human becoming that babies are involved in are so tightly woven that they deserve a degree of examination that is beyond the scope of this book. Alderson (2000) has a particularly interesting approach to this area.

─────────○ PART ONE

Human beings and human becomings

○───────────────────────────

In 1948 the General Assembly of the United Nations adopted and pro-claimed a Universal Declaration of Human Rights (see www.un.org). The signatories to the Declaration, including most of the countries of the world, agreed that all human beings, regardless of the political regime they lived under, had a number of basic rights and freedoms that no state could take away from them. Forty-one years later in 1989 the General Assembly adopted the UN Convention on the Rights of the Child. This provided a special range of rights for those under 18 years old. Why was an extra, special Convention needed for children? If the first declaration covered all humans, did it not cover human children along with human adults?

This division of international regulation reflects a widespread tendency to think of adults and children as fundamentally different types of humans. Qvortrup (1994) captures the nature of this division well when he describes it (critically) as one between adult 'human beings' and child 'human becomings'. The human being is, or should be, stable, complete, self-possessed and self-controlling. The human being is, or should be, capable of independent thought and action, an independence that merits respect. The human becoming, on the other hand, is changeable and incomplete and lacks the self-possession and self-control that would allow it the independence of thought and action that merits respect. The division between beings and becomings is that between the complete and independent and the incomplete and dependent.

In this first part we shall ask where this division between two types of humans came from and why it has such widespread plausibility. We shall find answers in the historical growth of two figures: the 'standard adult' that is understood to have all the properties of an independent human being, and the 'developmental state', which is a model of proper relations between states and their populations within which children are understood to have all the properties of human becomings. We shall argue that the plausibility of the being/becoming distinction rests on the social and economic conditions that gave rise to the standard adult and to the developmental state. Essentially then, we shall argue that the being/becoming division is a product of historical development and that, as such, it is open to change.

In Chapters 1 and 2 we shall chart the rise of standard adulthood and of the developmental state. But we shall also argue that, in recent years, global economic, political and social changes have begun to erode both of these figures. In the age of uncertainty that these changes are bringing about it is hard to believe in the standard image of adulthood, and relations between states and their populations are changing in a way that makes it harder to see children simply as human becomings.

In Chapter 3 we shall see that the effects of the age of uncertainty have not gone unnoticed. Sociologists of childhood have tried to give expression to the erosion of the being/becoming distinction and to put our understanding of childhood on a new footing. They have argued that we should see children as beings alongside adults rather than as becomings in distinction from adults because children deserve respect and recognition in their own right. In short, they have argued that the category 'human becoming' should be emptied and abandoned. As we shall see, however, the erosion of our principal image of human being – the standard adult – makes it hard nowadays to see what 'being' means.

In summary then, this part will give an account of the historical emergence and contemporary erosion of the being/becoming division. It will also raise the question of how we are to understand childhood when both our human categories are coming under question.

①

What do you want to be when you grow up?

○──

Introduction: journey's end?

A division is often drawn between adult 'human beings' and child 'human becomings'. As we have already seen, children and adults would seem to be fundamentally different types of humans, requiring different sorts of global regulation. How are we to account for the existence and widespread credibility of this division? In this chapter we shall build half an answer to this by giving an account of the circumstances that have made it possible to think of adults as stable, complete human beings. But we shall also begin to draw the contours of our 'age of uncertainty', arguing that at the beginning of the twenty-first century widespread economic and cultural changes are eroding this understanding of the nature of adulthood.

A few decades ago there were very good reasons for thinking of adulthood as a state of personal stability and completion. Once an adult had a stable job and a stable intimate relationship, there would be very few significant changes in their life, except, perhaps, for having children. Even though many adults did not attain this level of stability in their lives, such stability still had the status of a norm or a guiding model of adult maturity. Against this backdrop of a stable, predictable adulthood, one's early life could be understood as a period in which one built toward that stability, secure in the assumption that it would arrive. Childhood, then, could be viewed as a journey towards a clear and *knowable* destination. But, as we enter the twenty-first century, the experience of adult life is a lot less stable than it used to be. With regard to being 'grown up', we have entered an age of uncertainty, an age in which adult life is newly unpredictable and in which whatever stabilities we manage to produce cannot be expected to last our whole lives.

This change in the experience of adulthood is of central importance to the social study of childhood because after some decades of adult stability, we had grown used to making sense of childhood *through* adulthood, interpreting everything children do, or have done to them, in terms of how this will affect their journey toward adulthood, or in terms of what it might tell us about how far a given child has travelled. Children's lives and activities *in the present* are still envisaged, in the main, as a preparation for the future. This peculiar dependence of thought about children on a picture of adulthood is reflected in the conceptual frameworks that, to this day, still dominate research into children and childhood. The ideas of 'socialization' and 'development', for example, carry that sense of childhood as a journey toward a destination. A sense of certainty about adulthood and its stability has been the rock on which social scientific knowledge of childhood is built.

As long as adulthood could be treated as a fixed point that everybody understood, childhood could be defined in relation to this certainty. Thus, children were often defined as whatever adults were *not*. Where adults were stable and mostly unchanging over time, children, as they grew up, were going through many changes. This made them, by nature, unstable and incomplete. Where adults' stability and completeness are understood to allow them to act in society, to participate independently in serious activities like work and politics, children's instability and incompleteness mean that they are often understood only as dependent and passive recipients of adults' actions. The clear contrast between adulthood and childhood, between beings and becomings, meant that it was hard to understand children as persons in their own right.

But now the permanent jobs and permanent relationships that made adulthood look like a state of stability are not so widely available. As we shall see, twenty-first-century adults have to adapt to, and remain adaptable to, a world that is full of the promise and threat of rapid change, both at work and in their intimate lives. Change and incompleteness have entered adulthood as principles for living that replace stability and completeness. In other words, one of the main bases for the clear contrast between adulthood and childhood is being eroded. Journey's end is receding from view and, thus, can no longer be relied upon to make sense of childhood. The implications of this destabilization of adulthood are vitally important for understanding contemporary relationships of authority and power between adults and children.

Standard adulthood: deviant childhood

We have already noted that childhood has been defined in opposition to adulthood. Growing up, then, is often taken to be a process in which something (a child) turns into its opposite (an adult), a process in which the boundary between becoming and being is crossed. But how can something turn into its opposite? How can one type of human turn into another type of human? Perhaps we have become used to thinking of adulthood as journey's end because the process of growing up presents itself as a riddle. Perhaps the idea that adults and children are in some way fundamentally different, adults being complete while children are incomplete, was always just a convenient fiction, a quick and easy way of avoiding confusion. If so, then it has proved a fiction of extraordinary power and utility. If we can convince ourselves that we know what we as adults are like, then it makes it easier for us to decide how far a given child has to go before counting as a person in their own right, deserving of rights, responsibilities and recognition. Adulthood, with all its connotations of stability and completeness, has operated as a kind of standard model of a person, which stands ready to be used to measure children's incompleteness. This process of measurement underlies, and acts as a justification for, many distributions of power and authority in society along lines of age and maturity. To take a simple example, across the democratic world, the right to vote in elections is withheld from many young people on the grounds that they are not yet competent to make such important decisions. The rights of full citizenship are distributed according to a logic of maturation that assumes that adults, simply by virtue of having attained the age of majority, are competent to make such decisions.

What happens, then, to the question of whether adults themselves match up to the image of the 'standard adult'? When it comes to adults, the question is, more often than not, forgotten. Because adults are of a certain age, they stand safely outside its terms of reference. Chronological age can serve as a cloak of invisibility that conceals adults' shortcomings. So it looks like we sometimes simply forget to use the standard model of adulthood to ask questions about adults. But, just as often, questions of how well adults match up to the image of the standard adult, and of whether indeed a given adult has reached 'journey's end' become buried in the number and urgency of other issues that, as adults, we feel the responsibility to address. Among the many other kinds of work that adults do, they are also often engaged in the work of making decisions about children and about how they are to live, particularly when they are acting as caregivers, childcare and educational professionals or public policy-makers. Sometimes adults make decisions on behalf of children, or in children's 'best interests'. Sometimes adults even make decisions about whether children are capable of making decisions for themselves or of formulating valuable opinions about how their lives should be.

This tells us something rather important. The images of journey's end, and of the standard adults who are taken to have arrived at journey's end, are crucial in maintaining the authority that adults often have over children, the right and duty to make decisions for them. Our convenient fictions about adulthood are of greatest use when we are exerting that authority or facing the responsibilities toward children that adulthood brings with it. In other words, the way we go about defining adulthood and childhood and the way we discriminate in our decision-making between adults and children is closely tied to the distribution of authority and power between age groups. If we forget to test adults against a standard, then that forgetting is distinctly 'motivated'. Much authority is distributed on the basis of age, and this distribution is itself supported by the notion that children do not match up in their competences to the standard adult. Journey's end and standard adulthood are 'convenient' fictions, then, only in cases where we would wish to preserve the existing age-based distributions of authority in society.

Some commentators think that there are very good reasons for challenging existing distributions of power and authority between adults and children. We shall be discussing their arguments in greater detail in Chapter 3. In the mean time, we ought to note that one of these reasons is that adults do not always use their power and authority well. The more one is in a position to make decisions for children, to speak on their behalf, the more one is able to silence their voices. Abusive, cruel or unfair treatment of children can hide behind this wall of silence.

So far, then, we have seen that adult authority over children, the ability of adults to speak for children and to make decisions on their behalf, has been supported by the image of the standard adult. We have also briefly noted that there are good reasons to be suspicious of the degree of authority that adults have, and that, in the light of these suspicions, adult authority has become controversial. But beneath this controversy, widespread social changes have been taking place that are bringing those forgotten questions of whether adults match up to the image of the standard adult to the fore. In fact, these changes are eroding standard adulthood. Over the past few decades, changes in working lives and in intimate relationships have cast the stability and completeness of adults into doubt and made it difficult and, often, undesirable for adults to maintain such stability. We shall shortly explore some of those changes in adulthood in greater detail. We shall see that as the social conditions that allowed adulthood to seem stable and complete are eroded, it is becoming harder to identify adulthood with stability and completeness.

Flexible adults in an age of uncertainty

We have portrayed the connection that is often made between adulthood and stability as a convenient fiction. But we should not imagine that this image of adulthood lacks any material support, or that we have grown used to thinking of adulthood as journey's end by sheer accident. Rather, we need to discover what social and economic arrangements have, over the twentieth century, made such a view of adulthood credible. We shall see that this image of standard adulthood was supported by specific patterns in the organization of people's working lives and in the organization of their intimate relationships. Once we have laid out the social and economic context in which the nature of adulthood seemed certain and obvious, we can then turn to describe the changes in social and economic arrangements that are making adulthood uncertain today. We need to begin with a little economic history.

From Fordist adulthood to flexible adulthood

Harvey (1989) describes the shape of national economies and patterns of work that were prevalent between the end of the Second World War (1945) and the early 1970s as 'Fordist'. The term derives from the name of Henry Ford, the founder of the Ford motor-car manufacturing company. Ford founded his company in 1914 in the USA on certain principles of organization that were not normally applied in motor-car manufacture at that time. Up until Ford, cars were a luxury commodity, built one at a time by small teams of craftsmen in small businesses. Ford introduced principles of *mass production* to the manufacture of cars. By breaking the process of car manufacture down into many small, simple steps, by spreading these steps along an assembly line, and by setting large numbers of employees to the repetition of these small simple steps, Fordist production methods allowed for a great increase in the number of cars that could be produced per employee, and an increase in the efficient use of each employee's time. By making many cars at one time, rather than one at a time, Ford's methods allowed his business to enjoy economies of scale, such as reductions in costs of raw materials for bulk purchasing and the ability to use and reuse expensive tools and manufacturing plant many times. This meant that Ford could produce many identical standardized cars at a relatively competitive price. Ford's strategy, then, involved large factories employing many people. It took considerable investment to start this business up. Ford had to make long-term plans and financial commitments in order to build large enough factories to employ enough people to profit from efficiencies of the assembly line and economies of scale.

During the Second World War, and in the wave of post-war economic reconstruction that followed, Fordist principles of production were adopted in key industrial regions around the globe. From the west Midlands of Britain to the Tokyo-Yokohama region of Japan (Harvey 1989: 132), Fordist mass production became the standard model of 'blue-collar' manual work. As long as Fordist businesses continued to be profitable, employees could look forward to very stable conditions of employment. Once one had learnt one's task on the assembly line well enough to keep up with the pace of production, one need not seek to change one's range of skills. Further, since so much capital had been invested in the factory in which one worked, according to a long-term plan, one could feel relatively confident that one would continue to work in the same place and among more or less the same people until retirement. The sheer scale of Fordist production and the level of investment it required helped to stabilize employees' lives.

As Harvey (1989: 135) points out, Fordism, with its stability, reliability and standardization of products, was not just a business strategy, it was a 'total way of life'. This meant that the Fordist economy brought business, government and individual aspirations into alignment around goals of long-term political stability and economic growth. As a recipe for business success that would guarantee high levels of employment, Fordism attracted the support of many governments. For Fordism to provide those high levels of employment, it was necessary that markets for mass-produced goods be maintained. Wage levels needed to be high enough for the bulk of the population to afford the new range of consumer goods. Thus national governments became involved in making wage settlements between employers and employees. Across western Europe, developing welfare states gave ordinary people the sense of security against sickness, injury and unemployment needed for them to risk spending their wages on consumer goods like cars and refrigerators. The production and consumption of mass-produced goods were linked in a 'virtuous spiral' of increasing prosperity.

This picture of employment conditions in the post-war period has, so far, focused on blue-collar employees. But a similar motif of stability can be found in the careers and employment conditions of white-collar workers such as civil servants, office workers and managers between 1945 and the early 1970s. Arthur *et al.* (1999) draw on Galbraith (1971) to sketch what they refer to as the 'industrial state', a socio-economic arrangement that is quite similar to Harvey's Fordism. On their account, the idealized organization of this period was 'a large, stable hierarchical pyramid' (Arthur *et al.* 1999: 8) and the ideal worker was someone who would stay loyal to the organization, building a career by gradually climbing that pyramid. In pursuit of this ideal, in which stability and long-term planning worked to the mutual benefit of employee and organization, companies developed career planning systems to encourage staff to remain with the company. A stable workforce was something to be treasured. As employees aged, so their jobs became more secure, since they had built up a larger stock of valuable experience and expertise. It was certainly the case that white-collar workers, unlike blue-collar workers, were expected to add to their range of skills in order to progress through the hierarchy, but these changes were understood as minor additions to the worker's basic personality. Organizational career planning was largely based on the notion that each employee had highly stable psychological characteristics that suited them to one career path or another (Arthur *et al.* 1999).

In summary, between 1945 and the early 1970s across the industrialized world, economic arrangements between businesses, governments and employees were such that once one was in employment, one could reasonably expect that one's working conditions would remain stable. This meant that once 'adult' and employed, one could expect to stay 'the same' for the rest of one's life in a range of ways; one's identity was stabilized by sharing the work environment with more or less the same people throughout one's working life; the geographical area one lived in would remain the same since the organization one belonged to had set down firm roots in that area; and, even if one were dissatisfied with one's job, one would not have to seek a position with another organization (in another place with different people) because time and effort would bring the reward of career progression. These stabilities depended on the maintenance of Fordism's 'virtuous spiral' of mass production and mass consumption.

Our contemporary associations of adulthood with stability grew from this soil. For a great number of people whose working lives were organized along Fordist lines, the transition to adulthood, marked by getting a job with a large organization, actually was journey's end. Familiar faces and one's locality were quickly settled, on employment, along with the list of skills one would have to use at work until retirement. One important thing to note here, however, is that these stable adult lives were highly gendered. The majority of the Fordist workforce were men. We might begin to suspect, then, that the image of the standard adult who has reached journey's end is similarly gendered. We shall return to this shortly. For the moment we can move on to describe the changes that lay behind the rise of 'flexible' adulthood.

Though Fordism or the industrial state developed, spread and strengthened for nearly 30 years, defining a clear picture of adulthood and shaping expectations for generations, in the early 1970s this widespread socioeconomic and cultural preference for stability was to end. As we have seen, Fordist strategies for economic success had aligned the interests and activities of manufacturing industry, governments and the lifestyles and expectations of individuals. This alignment had been achieved through mass production for mass markets, markets which were themselves fostered and supported by government interventions in the setting of wage rates and the provision of welfare. But for Fordism to continue to deliver the benefits of stable adult lives within a stable and growing economy, it needed ever-expanding markets for its goods.

By the late 1960s the domestic markets of Fordist economies like those of the USA or the UK were reaching saturation point. The virtues of mass production were turning into the burden of over-production. At the same time the global marketplace was becoming more competitive. The newly industrialized nations of South East Asia had adopted the methods of mass production, but, principally because of lower wage costs, they were able to undercut western manufacturers and to intrude on their domestic markets. The large scales and long-term investments of Fordism acted as a brake on western businesses' ability to adapt their product designs and business practices in order to compete. In this new environment, what had seemed to be a valuable stability in the economy became a problematic *rigidity* (Harvey 1989: 142). Workforces' expectations of stable working conditions and national governments' policies for the stabilization of a domestic consumer base added to this rigidity. The 'virtuous spiral' of mass production and mass consumption became a 'vicious spiral' of inflation, recession and industrial disputes.

Over the course of the 1970s and 1980s, the western economies that had suffered from the collapse of Fordism were to reorganize in response to the changing conditions of the global economy. The response was to react against stability, for fear of becoming rigid. All that had been carefully stabilized and managed in accordance with long-term plans and expectations was rendered *flexible*. Why employ your whole workforce for a lifetime, when you could save on wage bills by employing them only when demand for your products was rising? All a flexible manufacturing business needed in order to thrive was a core of managerial staff, access to part-time and short-term contract workers and a group of other businesses – subcontractors – to buy services and parts from, as and when they were needed. Harvey (1989: 141) describes this new economic regime as 'flexible accumulation'. For Arthur *et al.* (1999: 8) it is simply the 'new economy'. In the new economy flexible manufacturing strategies have produced a new obligation for adults who want paid employment – be prepared to adapt at any time or find oneself economically dead. Arthur and Rousseau (1996) advocate the boundary-less career in which there is no loyalty between employer and employee, and in which the ideal employee moves frequently between employers taking the opportunity to develop a portfolio of new skills as they go.

Employment arrangements under 'flexible accumulation' can serve those adults who are ready to adapt and to be flexible quite well. It can also serve to punish those who are unwilling or unable to adapt or are simply unaware of the necessity to be adaptable. Either way, the stability in conditions of employment that allowed us to think of adults as intrinsically stable and to associate adulthood with stability and completeness, has been considerably eroded. So at the beginning of the twenty-first century, many adults are unsure about where, with whom and in what capacity they will be working in five years' time. It seems that the figure of the standard adult against which we still make judgements about children, the figure that still serves as the basis for adult authority over children, is a 'convenient' fiction that belongs to a Fordist past rather than a flexible present.

From roles to choices: flexibility in intimate life

So far we have seen that the image of the standard adult has played an important role in giving adults authority over children, and that adult 'stability' was a key element of that image. Economic and social change since the early 1970s has been turning one major source of that adult stability – the workplace – from a zone in which long-term certainty might be expected and experienced into a zone of flexibility that demands adaptability, willingness and ability to change from adults. We also noted that the Fordist standard adult, the figure whose life had been most effectively stabilized by large-scale hierarchical organization, tended to be male. The image of adult stability was not solely dependent on working conditions for its credibility. Stable adulthood was also generated in long-term intimate relationships such as marriages. As we shall see, recent decades have seen changes in this intimate sphere of life that are placing long-term relationship stabilities in question, just as the 'new economy' has rendered the workplace uncertain and adulthood 'flexible'.

The sociologist Talcott Parsons (1971) identified what he called the 'normal American family'. This 'normal' family was based on a monogamous marriage between a man and a woman and was expected to last until one or other partner died. The adult members of this stable unit lived together, shared their income and raised children. According to Parsons (1971), this way of organizing family life had developed from an earlier middle-class standard, and had spread across US society as prosperity increased in the course of the twentieth century. Decreases in mortality rates and increasingly widespread stable conditions of male employment meant that once a couple were living in such a 'normal' family, the only significant changes in their way of life would come with the birth and maturation of their children. This normal family, then, could be thought of as providing a stable context in which the instability and incompleteness of growing children could be safely and comfortably accommodated. For Parsons (1971) it was the stability of the adult intimate relationship within the normal family that allowed for the successful socialization of children. In other words, it was the stability of adults within the family that gave legitimacy to whatever authority adults wielded over their children.

Parsons' general picture of society relies heavily on the concept of 'role' (Parsons 1956), where a role reflects one's allotted place within the institutions of society. Whatever social institutions Parsons examined, he sought to identify the roles people occupied. The role one had determined the range of actions which were appropriate to you, and to a large extent governed the way you lived your life. It was clearly defined roles then, that were the key to social stability for Parsons. For each person, knowledge of their role reduced the amount of choice they had to exercise in their lives, and, if each person acted according to role, according to others' expectations of them, then confusion would be minimized, order would be maximized, and society would remain stable. For Parsons, 'growing up' equated to the socialization of children, during which process children gained knowledge of their and others' roles in society so as to allow for the reproduction of society's key institutions, not least the family. Ideally, each generation should pass on knowledge of roles and norms to the next. In Parsons' view of society the traditional patterns of the past were reproduced for the future through the family unit. Families were not just stable in themselves, built on traditional relationships of authority, they were also a major source of social stability in that they helped to reproduce traditional relationships of authority.

It is easy to see how Parsons' stable, clearly defined roles within stable families reflected the socio-economic conditions of Fordism. Rather like Ford's production-line employees, adults in intimate relationships had only to realize their roles and discharge their duties and responsibilities in order to secure a stable life and stable authority over their children. The normal family that Parsons identified was founded on just such a set of clear roles and mutual expectations. While male employment was relatively stable and long term, the adult male household role was to bring home the principal share of the family's income, while the adult female household role was, principally, to keep the house in order and to take care of any children. Likewise the roles of male and female children were to receive socialization from their parents, toward the end of taking up similar stable, gender-appropriate roles within stable marriages when they, in their turn, reached journey's end.

According to Giddens (1992), the degree of stability, certainty and conformity to roles that composed Parsons' 'normal' family was closely linked to what people of his time were looking for in intimate relationships. In the industrial west a dominant model of 'love' organized people's expectations as they sought and entered intimate relationships in young adulthood. This was 'romantic love'. From the nineteenth century onwards, to 'fall in love' was to have found a partner for the rest of one's life, a partner with whom one had a deep emotional and psychological affinity. On marriage, this affinity would form the basis of an emotional and economic union to last a lifetime. Ideally, money and mutual care were shared without reservation, and the degree of trust this sharing involved was secured by the knowledge that this relationship, being romantically founded on the stable emotional and psychological characters of the two partners, would last 'forever'.

Romance provided stability for the love relationship. Any conflicts or dissatisfactions attendant on the gendered division of labour in the household could be dissolved within the acknowledgement of mutual dependence and in the lifelong terms of the agreement of trust that such a relationship was founded on. The long-term stabilities of romantic love and the degree of clear separation of gender roles that it allowed were also offered support by the Fordist economic environment that sustained men as the principal economic actors in the family.

But on Giddens' (1992) view, romantic love can no longer claim to be the dominant principle of intimate relationships between adults. Across the western world it has been supplanted by a new ideal that he calls the 'pure relationship' (Giddens 1992: 58). The central difference between intimate relationships that are based on romantic love and those that are based on the pure relationship is that the latter are maintained only so long as they satisfy the needs of the persons involved. This does not mean that 'love' has disappeared. Rather a new form of love has emerged – 'confluent love' (Giddens 1992: 61). Love is understood to last just so long as it makes sense for each lover, just so long as they are both satisfied by it. As Smart and Neale (1999) write,

> The idea that one finds the right person and then stays committed to him or her through thick and thin is supplanted by the idea that if that person proves to be inadequate in some way, he or she can be replaced with a more suitable or compatible partner.
>
> (Smart and Neale 1999: 8)

If the standards of good relationships have indeed changed in this way, then intimate relationships can no longer automatically provide adults with a stability they can be sure of. One must negotiate and renegotiate one's relationship rather than take it for granted. In other words, one must be flexible. Adults no longer feel obliged to follow socially sanctioned standards of commitment or to live out roles that they have inherited from their parents. Indeed if one feels that one's partner is 'acting out a role', this might nowadays lead one to question the quality of the relationship. This change in people's expectations of their relationships has played its part in increasing divorce rates in the west (Smart and Neale 1999). But, just as significantly, even intimate relationships that *do* last are now forged against a backdrop of possible separation and in the knowledge of their potential instability.

What factors lie behind this shift from permanent romantic love rooted in tradition to contingent confluent love rooted in mutual satisfaction? We can look to recent economic change for an answer. The flexible 'new economy' means that one's geographical location, one's employment status, one's range of skills and, above all, one's self-identity now remain open to change. It might seem that the flexibility of today's intimate relationships is the direct result of flexible working conditions. But as Castells (1997) argues, the sources of change in intimate life are more diverse than this. He places the increased availability of birth control, the increasing visibility of gay and lesbian relationships, and, most importantly for us, the global development of feminism since the 1970s, alongside economic change in explaining the increasingly flexible nature of intimate relationships.

Standard adulthood and gender

We have already noted that stable Fordist adulthood, based on long-term unchanging employment conditions, was more an experience of men than one of women. If many men's experience of labour throughout their lives was a more or less smooth and uninterrupted passage through well-planned pathways, represented by the blue-collar assembly line or the white-collar career path, women's experience was quite different. Traditional gender roles placed married women in the home and charged them with the responsibility of actively producing stability in the home for men and for children, by (among many other things) preparing regular meals, keeping the house tidy, and attending to children's emotional and practical needs. So while men had stabilities made *for them* at work and at home, women had to create stability *for others*. Further, women's access to stable lifelong employment was compromised by childbirth. If the Fordist workplace gave stability to employees' lives it also required employees to be available for work throughout their lives without interruption. The Fordist workplace was not designed with childbirth in mind and thus tended to exclude women from the workforce.

For these reasons then, women under Fordism did not have easy access to the stabilities of standard adulthood. It was difficult for a woman who was a wife and mother also to be a standard adult. The degree to which a woman could be an economically independent person was limited by her financial dependence on her male partner. The degree to which she could pass as a complete and stable person was limited by her continual involvement in producing stabilities for others. If children, by comparison with adults, were non-standard persons, then, because of their socio-economic position, adult women were non-standard too.

The feminist movement of the late 1960s and 1970s was a range of different protests against the values and socio-economic arrangements that effectively excluded women from the status, powers and privileges of standard adulthood. Living in a world that was designed to produce stability, security and authority for adult men tended to produce frustration and anger for many women. The feminist movement gathered women and their experiences of exclusion together and, over time, made these once purely 'personal' matters 'political', that is to say, available for public discussion and recognition. Once women's discontents with the normal family and all that surrounded and supported it were a matter of public record, it became possible to see that whatever arrangement had been struck upon within an intimate relationship was open to negotiation and revision as circumstances and individuals aspirations changed. By criticizing existing standards and norms, and by building alternative standards and norms (such as gender equality within the home), feminism opened the terms and conditions of intimate relationships to factors of preference and choice.

In the confluent pattern of relationships that has resulted, the stability of the intimate relationship is not taken for granted. If it is achieved at all, it is achieved on a provisional basis through the flexibility of partners and their openness to changing their lifestyles. Ideally, such flexible intimacy should equally accommodate the desires and aspirations of both male and female partners. We should note for the sake of clarity that it is not at all necessary for such relationships to be based on a clear understanding of, or commitment, to feminist politics. Flexible adulthoods in intimate life arise simply because people's intimate lives are now lived with the sense that there are always alternatives. In stark contrast to Parsons' (1971) picture of society, the past is no longer a reliable guide to the present or, for that matter, to the future. More reliable birth control methods and a growing awareness of the viability of gay and lesbian intimate relationships have only added to this sense of choice and provisionality in intimate life (Castells 1997). Today models of the family based on 'traditional stability' and 'flexible choice' are in conflict across the world. In the industrial west, political debate about social policy has become fixated on the issue of 'traditional family values' as more egalitarian relationships between men and women are developing (Risman 1998). For Castells (1997), many of the present-day Christian, Muslim and Jewish 'fundamentalist' movements are primarily concerned with preserving traditional parental authority (most often paternal authority) against a global tide of flexibility, diversity and choice.

Conclusion: adulthood, authority and the age of uncertainty

We have seen how important the assumption of the stability of adulthood and adult lives has been in distributing authority between age groups. The 'finished' standard adult has powers over and responsibilities toward the 'unfinished' child. We have also seen that this assumption of finished stability no longer holds good in either adults' working lives or in their intimate relationships. Indeed, this model of stability has only ever been fully available to men, just less than half the adult population. So let us now outline the consequences of the changes we have described for the place of children in society as they grow up in this age of uncertainty.

The destabilization of adulthood in the sphere of intimate life is eroding the traditional basis of parents' authority over their children. As flexibility has become a basic principle of intimate adult relationships, the reproduction of traditional roles has become a less important feature of family life. As long as tradition and the reproduction of roles was more important than choice, flexibility and negotiation in shaping the family, then adults, simply by virtue of having greater experience of the past than their children, could enjoy the status of *experts* on how to live. Parents could rely on always 'knowing better' than their children, and their superior knowledge and understanding was given institutional support in the form and functions of the family. Along with their responsibility to raise their children to fit into society came a legitimate and well-grounded authority over their children. Though the sense that adults have greater experience than their children has not disappeared (far from it) it is less likely today, especially in the industrial west, to translate directly into parents' ability to command children's obedience. Beck (1998: 65) sums up the significance of these changes with the phrase 'the democratisation of the family', which suggests a future in which children as much as parents may become actively involved in shaping their families through negotiation and participation in decision-making.

As adulthood is led into flexibility by socio-economic and cultural change across the globe, it is clear that stable, complete, standard adulthood can no longer be presumed to exist. It can no longer be relied upon to form the basis of our understanding of childhood and, as we have seen most clearly in the case of intimate relationships, it can no longer form the basis of adult authority over children. The fictional aspect of the 'standard adult' is fast outgrowing its convenience. Uncertainty over the nature of childhood and uncertainty over how properly to treat children is emerging just as the capstone of standard adulthood is lifted from societies across the globe. To give a sense of the issues that now confront us, we end this chapter with the following quotation:

Modern parents know a lot about children and child development as compared with previous generations. Still, many of them simply feel at a loss at what to do. They listen eagerly to the advice of experts, but soon discover they often change their minds and prove themselves to be unreliable . . . Nobody can give hard and fast advice, the know-how changes just as quickly as the development itself. Uncertainty is chronic.

(Dencik 1989: 174)

2

Defining the dependent child

○───────────────────────────────────────

In the previous chapter, we saw how relationships between adults and children have been influenced by understandings of adulthood as a state of stable completeness and of childhood as a state of unstable incompleteness. For a time, it was quite obvious that adulthood and childhood were, in this sense, opposites. It was possible to arrange relationships between the two kinds of persons according to their clear oppositional categorization. Thus, as we have seen, adults not only provided for children, but also decided for children and spoke for them. We saw that this oppositional conception of adults and children was supported by patterns of employment and intimate relationships within which a picture of adulthood as journey's end was credible. So Chapter 1 gave half of our explanation of the widespread credibility of the categorical difference between 'human beings' and 'human becomings'.

We also argued, however, that in the latter decades of the twentieth century, adult lives became more flexible, and adulthood became less stable and less complete. As flexibility enters adult life in our age of uncertainty, it is becoming harder to see children and adults as opposites. It is becoming increasingly difficult to justify forms of adult authority over children that depend on the clear distinction between adult and child. In this chapter we shall complete our account of the widespread credibility and application of the being/becoming divide. We shall move on from issues of adult stability and completeness to ask how the young came to be identified as incomplete and dependent, how, in other words, the category of 'human becoming' arose.

We have already seen that throughout the twentieth century, understandings of childhood had been dependent on understandings of adulthood. As childhood was revealed as unstable, and thus uncertain, it became something of a mystery, needing to be defined and held in place by a capstone of certain adulthood. Childhood could be known, but only by reference to a standard adulthood. In other words, not only were children dependent on adults – reliant on them to discharge their care-giving responsibilities properly – but also, in the twentieth century the very idea of childhood itself was dependent on a conception of adulthood. So where did such a deep sense of childhood dependency come from? Did it emerge only in the twentieth century alongside the Fordist national economies and the patterns of intimate family relationships that they sustained?

We are going to suggest that the story of childhood dependency is more complex than this. We shall argue that childhood became associated with dependency long before the notion of adulthood as journey's end developed. By the time intimate and working relations were being shaped by Fordism, by the time Parsons' (1971) 'normal' family was becoming the norm, the notion of childhood dependency was already available to feed into the coordination of family, state and business practices that emerged during Fordism. We shall see that the condition of dependent childhood is just as closely tied to the fate of nation-states and the plans of governments as the twentieth century's standard adulthoods were. In the course of this chapter, then, we shall argue that childhood dependency emerged alongside the development of European nation-states from the seventeenth to the nineteenth centuries. As European states defined themselves through mutual military and economic competition and through colonization of other parts of the world, arrangements for the care and upbringing of children became a key focus of concern and intervention. Such states were 'developmental states' in the sense that they were concerned to shape their citizens as they grew up to become persons fit for state purposes and ambitions. Childhood became identified as a site of investment for the future, a future which states were keen to control. Thus, techniques for intervening in childhood were developed as means to intervene in the future of the state. It was through this model of the developmental state that childhood became identified with dependency.

The investment in children by the developmental state reached its peak in the industrial west under Fordism. But, as we have already suggested in our coverage of the 'new economy' (Arthur *et al.* 1999), change continues apace. In the global, flexible economy, states are experiencing a reduction of their autonomy and of their powers to control their own future (Castells 1997). So in this chapter we shall also explore the issue of how more recent changes in the powers of states are giving children an identity as dependants that can be held in *independence* of states. We shall argue that 'dependency' itself is becoming ambiguous in its implications for children. First, however, we need to make some preliminary points about dependency.

Dependencies: necessary and accidental

To the extent that one is dependent, one must rely upon the assistance, goodwill and competence of others. Dependence varies in degree from partial and specific forms to total and general forms. Lacking a specific skill, one may need another's assistance to complete a single task. In such cases, one's dependence is partial and specific. If engaged in a joint enterprise, one may require constant and lasting assistance from another in order to bring that enterprise to completion. This is an instance of dependence generalized over time. Total dependence would include instances of physical incapacity where one needs others' help simply to stay alive. It is clear, then, that to some extent or other, adults and children both have dependencies. But a distinction that is often drawn between adulthood and childhood, is that adulthood is a state of independence while childhood is a state of dependence. Even though it is clear that no adult is entirely independent of others, when we compare adults and children, we are somehow able to discount instances of adult dependence. Just as we can forget to compare real adults against the image of the standard adult (see Chapter 1), so when considering the relationship between adulthood and childhood, we can forget how much help adults need from other people in their daily lives. What, then, allows us to forget or to discount instances of adult dependence?

Alongside variations in degree of dependence, another discrimination is at work, a discrimination between accidental and necessary forms of dependence. Though an adult might require assistance, and require it often, this is generally understood to be due to the circumstances they find themselves in rather than due to the kind of person they are. Adults, it seems, can move in and out of dependency as they move through social life. This means that each instance of their dependence can be discounted as accidental or circumstantial. Instances of children's dependence, however, seem to be closely tied to the kind of people they are. Rather than passing in and out of states of dependency, a child carries dependency with themselves. So, if a child needs assistance, this is understood to be because they are a dependent kind of person. Dependence, then, is lodged within the image of childhood that follows children through social life. This image of childhood ensures that a series of different instances of a particular child's need for others' assistance can be added up as cumulative evidence of the child's dependent nature, while instances of a particular adult's need for assistance do not accumulate in this way. Thus, children's participation in social life tends to be interpreted through dependence, while adults' participation in social life tends to be interpreted through independence.

Now it might be argued that this striking difference in the 'mathematics' of dependency between the categories 'adult' and 'child' arises because children are in some sense *naturally* dependent. Indeed, children's dependency and the consequent set of obligations of protection and care that adults have towards them, in their various roles as caregivers, friends and relatives, seem very well founded. It would, to use a crude example, take a considerable and questionable feat of mental gymnastics to produce good reasons why a parent should *not* warn a small child of the dangers presented by an open fire. In many cases, then, the notion that children personally depend on specific adults for protection is nothing more than good sense. Perhaps the most basic sense of children's dependency arises from the observation that, compared with most adults, most children are physically weak. They would indeed need the personal protection of a strong adult if confronted by another who was physically attacking or intimidating them.

The link between childhood and dependency, however, carries well beyond personal relationships of physical protection. As things stand, children are often economically dependent on adults to feed and clothe them, dependent on adults to make many important decisions for them, and dependent on adults to socialize them if they are, in due course, to become fully fledged members of society. Thus many of the ways in which children are socially defined as dependent have little or no direct connection with physical weakness. Further, many of the relationships of dependency that children find themselves in are institutional in character, regulated and planned for many people, rather than purely personal matters of individual relationships. Many of the obligations that adults have toward children are supported, for example, by legal regulation; children's economic dependence, for example, is enforced in some countries by the strict regulation and limitation of children's labour. Likewise, parents' conduct toward their children can be scrutinized by state agencies to determine whether they are taking care of their children properly (Parton 1985).

Given both the range and institutional character of these forms of dependence, it is unlikely that children's relative vulnerability to physical attack can fully justify or account for the identification of childhood with dependency. Physical vulnerability for example provides no explanation of children's apparent dependence on adults to make decisions on their behalf. States of dependency, it would seem, are *socially* distributed rather than ordained by facts of physical size and strength. So how is it that children are defined in so many ways as dependent? How is it that childhood and dependency are so closely identified with one another? Why are so many activities undertaken on children's behalf rather than by children themselves, and why is so much attention devoted to regulating the relationship between adults and their dependants? To answer these questions, we must examine the development of the institutions and practices through which childhood has become identified with dependency.

In the following section, we shall argue that the equation of childhood and dependence has deep historical roots. The apparent inevitability of childhood's dependency is neither the result of any simple fact of physical weakness nor the result of some simple error of over-generalization from ideas of personal physical protection to institutionalized dependency. Rather, the various forms of children's contemporary dependency and the way that children are taken to carry dependency with them through social life are intimately connected with the form and functions of the modern state. The equation of childhood with dependency is a result of the growth of the *developmental state* as an ideal template for relationships between individual adults, adult authorities and children.

Modernity and 'garden cultures'

We begin our account of the identification of childhood with dependency by examining the development of a model of the relationship between rulers and the ruled, a model that involves deliberate planned investment in the lives of the ruled population on the part of the rulers. The roots of this model lie in seventeenth-century western Europe, but in the course of the eighteenth and nineteenth centuries it was to spread, sometimes by emulation, sometimes by coercion, to many other parts of the world (Bauman 1987). The application of this model contributed to the formation of the nation-state as a political and economic entity. As we shall see, it was within this model that children came to be identified as 'dependent'.

Bauman (1987: 51) describes the relationship between the rulers and the ruled of European societies before the seventeenth century through the metaphor of 'gamekeeping'. The job of the gamekeeper is to ensure that the population of animals on a stretch of land is kept at the right levels to sustain hunting for food and for sport. To do this, the gamekeeper needs to intervene in the environment only in certain limited ways. If the population of carnivorous animals grows too large, the number of birds and small mammals is likely to drop below the levels required for food. In these circumstances the gamekeeper may selectively cull some of those carnivores, to keep the level of food animals high. Likewise, if the number of, say, rabbits starts to increase rapidly, threatening the growth of vegetation and the population of game-birds who need that vegetation for shelter, the gamekeeper may set traps for them to reduce their numbers. The game-keeper's activities, then, are oriented toward the preservation of a balanced environment. Apart from selective culling and trapping, however, the game-keeper makes few interventions in the lives of animals and plants. The gamekeeper is not required, for example, to supply rabbits or game-birds with food stuffs or medicines. As a strategy for managing land, game-keeping, to a large extent, leaves the land to its own devices. It relies on animals' and plants' own ability to reproduce themselves and to stay in good health.

For Bauman (1987), the relationship between pre-modern rulers and the populations they had power over was like that between gamekeepers and the plants and animals of the land they kept. Like the gamekeeper, they had confidence in their 'trustee's natural resourcefulness' (Bauman 1987: 52). They relied upon the population's own ability to reproduce itself, to pass on the skills of farming and production of goods from one generation to another, and, likewise, to pass on the customs and traditions that made for social stability. As 'gamekeepers', rulers' interventions were limited to securing 'a share in the wealth of goods these timeless habits produce[d]' (Bauman 1987: 52).

But as populations increased, as towns and cities grew, and as rulers embarked on the colonization of other lands far from home, their attitude toward the ruled began to change. Where, previously, gamekeeping could be relied upon to secure food, goods, skills and social order, the increasing needs of the ruled, coupled with the colonial ambitions of rulers, meant that more was required of the population. Why leave the population to its own devices when traditional ways of life were not productive enough? Former gamekeepers sought to turn themselves into 'gardeners' (Bauman 1987). Unlike the gamekeeper, the gardener approaches the land with objectives and plans that the land's own resourcefulness cannot satisfy. Gardeners aim to shape the land to their own purposes, extracting the maximum benefit from the population. Gardeners intervene at each stage of growth, taking deliberate control over the kinds of plants that flourish, training and feeding them to maximize their yield, and weeding out competing species that have no place in their design. Gardeners have a plan for an ideal garden and have strategies for making that plan come to life. The rulers of modernizing states thought of their population as a resource, just like pre-modern rulers. But they thought of that resource as being in need of shaping, training and controlling, as in need of calculated intervention and investment, because, in a concern for economic and military competition, they had discovered a new purpose for their states – to grow, to develop and to expand into the future.

Bauman (1987) lists a number of interventions that characterize the 'gardening' attitude of the rulers of modernizing states. Certain traditional practices, such as the holding of local festivals, became identified as wasteful of resources, encouraging drunkenness, laziness and crime among the people. Attempts were made to eliminate or to regulate them. Those who embodied traditional peasant wisdom, such as 'old wives' (Bauman 1987: 71), were identified as spreading ignorance and superstition and were persecuted as witches. Even old proverbs and folk sayings were targeted as crude, unrefined and irrational to the extent that they represented the resourcefulness of the ruled. But, for our purposes, the most significant feature of the shift from gamekeeping to gardening was the emergence of the notion that the population was in need of *education*. For the populations of modernizing states to play their part in the new plans of their rulers, traditional ways of living had to be eliminated and replaced with more rational and cultivated ways of living that were more compatible with the purpose of uniting the efforts of the population in states' interests. These ideas allowed rulers to assume the 'right and duty . . . to form its citizens and guide their conduct' (Bauman 1987: 69).

Though 'education' of one form or another has existed since antiquity, usually being provided only for the wealthy few, the modern form of education was quite distinctive in purpose and practice. It was conceived of as a tool to rescue the population from ignorance and ill-disciplined conduct and to turn them into a disciplined force whose every action would add to the strength of the state. In so far as the population held on to their traditions and their own resourcefulness, then, from the perspective of the rulers, they were incomplete and deficient whether child or adult. Though the proponents of this form of education often saw a need to train the entire population, it was the young who received most attention. The spirit of educational investment in the young for the benefit of the state and the degree of training they were thought to require is captured well in the following quote from Maximilien Robespierre, one of the authors of the French Revolution. In the ideal school, children would be:

> Constantly under the eyes and in the hands of an active surveillance, every hour will be marked as one of sleep, eating, work, exercise, rest; the whole order of life will be invariably regulated . . . A salutary and uniform regulation will prescribe every detail, and its constant and easy enforcement will guarantee good effects . . . A new, strong, industrious, orderly and disciplined race [will be created] separated by an impenetrable wall from all impure contact with the prejudices of our ancient species.
>
> (Bauman 1987: 73)

So far, then, we have learned that as states began to form as competing economic and military powers, a new relationship was forged between rulers and ruled. In this new relationship, the quality and conduct of the population was conceived of as being open to control and management; this control would take place partly through programmes of education; and, such interventions in the lives of the ruled, especially the young, were deemed necessary for the future success of the state. As they came to behave like gardeners, rulers identified the investment in and training of the young as a central concern of statesmanship. The young were being identified as embodiments of the future and, thus, as in need of special treatment. The modern state was a 'developmental state'. Reasons of state guided the treatment of children. It was in the interests of the state that children be separated from any sources of influence that might disturb the investments being made in them. The special place of the young in the developmental state gave rise to new classes of experts on children's well-being and development, experts apparently well placed to give advice on how to preserve children from the present for the sake of the future. In the following section, we shall see how these attitudes and practices of investment contributed to the isolation of children from mainstream society and gave rise to a general equation of childhood and dependency.

The preservation of children

Donzelot (1979) offer us an account of the development of the modern western conception of the family. He broadly shares Bauman's (1987) view of modernization as the development of practices designed to replace traditional ways of life with highly organized and 'rational' ways of managing the ruled, oriented to the production of a strong, industrious, orderly and disciplined population. But Donzelot (1979) makes this case through a close study of the changing relationships between the French state, new classes of child experts, and families, between the eighteenth and twentieth centuries. He focuses on the family as a functional element of the modern 'gardening' mode of government. In brief, his argument is that, if the example of France is anything to go by, the modern western family is the result of interactions between the demands of the developmental state, the activities, plans and wishes of family members and the knowledges produced by experts on the well-being and development of children. Along the way, he provides us with insights into how children's special place as sites of investment within the developmental state ensured that they were gradually separated from mainstream society. Our argument in this section will be that this growing separation set the conditions for our contemporary vision of children as fundamentally dependent becomings.

The sections of Donzelot's (1979) argument that are of particular concern to us focus on discussions around and practical responses to two ways of treating children that were common in mid-eighteenth-century France: the use of 'foundling' hospitals as a repository for orphaned and abandoned children and the employment of domestic nurses to raise children in wealthier homes. In each case, eighteenth-century commentators argued that these practices were bad for the children concerned, therefore bad for France as a state. In each case, alternative practices were advocated that were under-stood as better suited to the purpose of producing a strong, healthy and useful future population.

An orphaned or abandoned infant in mid-eighteenth-century France was liable to be placed in a 'foundling hospital' (Donzelot 1979: 9). Here they would be fed and clothed at state expense. The mortality rate in such hospitals, however, was very high. According to Donzelot's (1979) sources, anything up to 90 per cent of such foundlings would die while in state care. Criticism of these foundling hospitals was not made solely on the bases we contemporary observers might expect, such as a humanitarian concern for the well-being of children or the sentiment of pity for betrayed dependants. Rather, the vexation was that not only was money being wasted in such inefficient institutions, but so was the contribution that foundling children might make to France in the future. The death of children in state care was an affront to the rational principles of 'social economy' (Donzelot 1979: 12), principles that would see children primarily as investments, as embodiments of the future of the state. There was no shortage of suggestions of how better to manage the foundling problem. Notable among these was the following:

> Being without parents, with no other support than that obtained for them by wise government, they hold to nothing and have nothing to lose. Could death itself appear as something to be feared by such men as these, whom nothing seems to attach to life, and who could be accustomed to danger at an early age? It should not be difficult to make such people look upon death and danger with indifference when they are brought up without these sentiments and are not distracted by

any mutual tenderness. They will be equally well-suited to serve as sailors, to supplement the militia, or to populate colonies.

(Claude-Humbert Piarron de Chamousset,
cited in Donzelot 1979: 10)

The author's suggestion was, effectively, that male children be sent from the foundling hospitals to new military training institutions, the purpose of which was to raise them to be without fear of their own death, and without concern for the death of others, in order to further the military and colonial ambitions of the state. Rather than be exposed to the failings of existing institutions, they should be isolated from mainstream society, so that they might be preserved against common 'sentiments' and thus trained for specific purposes. The people most often blamed for the high mortality rates were the women employed to take care of foundlings. Coming from the countryside, or from the ranks of the urban poor, these women were easily identified with old-fashioned, traditional ways of raising children. In their distance from civilized ways, and in their ignorance of reasons of state, it seemed that these were quite the wrong people to have influence over the young.

The same rural or working-class women who were identified as the enemy of state progress in the foundling hospitals posed another problem in the houses of the wealthy. It was common practice for wealthy mothers to employ them to look after their children. Once again they were found to be at the root of any defects that the children might have, moulding children to their uncivilized ways:

One is sometimes surprised to see the children of upright and virtuous parents display, from their earliest years, a fundamental baseness and malice. We can be certain that it is from their nurses that these children derive all their vices. They would have been decent if their mothers had nursed them.

(William Buchan, cited in Donzelot 1979: 11)

On this view, the children of the wealthy were at risk from exposure to the bad influence of household servants. The proposed solutions to this problem came in many forms but were often to be found in publications written by medics. Such books of advice on child-rearing offered wealthy mothers alternatives to their servants' traditional ideas on child-rearing, and equipped them to combat these bad influences. Particular attention was given to outlining the dangers of the traditional practice of 'swaddling' infants (binding them so as to restrict their movements) and the telling of ghost stories. In this hygienist literature, it was taken to be the mother's job either to raise children herself in the light of expert advice on child-rearing, or, if that was not possible, to set up lines of defence within the home to protect her children's development from their nurse. This was to be achieved by the mother carefully choosing servants, and then being sure to keep a close eye on them and their childcare practices. The child was in need of protection from the base elements of society even when, indeed especially when, these base elements were to be found within the home. The protection of children combined mothers and new classes of experts on family life and child development against a common enemy – the household servants who embodied ignorance, superstition and tradition. In a context where there were clear ideas about the future usefulness of the growing child, then, the children of the wealthy came to be understood as dependent on mothers and on expert advice for protection from a contaminating world.

The policies that were to surround poorer families took a different form, but served the same end of isolating children from bad influences. From the late eighteenth century to the mid-nineteenth century charitable societies devoted to strengthening the institution of marriage proliferated (Donzelot 1979). The fewer the numbers of illegitimate or abandoned children and the greater the degree to which fathers brought income to stable family units, the smaller the expense to the state. But since these parents were of the unenlightened classes, guidance had to be provided for them, lest they raise their children in inappropriate ways. Thus family allowances, introduced in France at the end of the nineteenth century, were coupled with medical state supervision of working-class child-rearing (Donzelot 1979: 177).

The preservation of children, then, was broad in its effects. It turned families, both rich and poor, into sites for the defence of children against the ignorance and insufficiencies of mainstream society, represented principally by working-class women. As children came to be seen as embodiments of the future, so their susceptibility to bad influences became clear and their dependence on mothers, child-rearing experts and the existence of a stable family home became obvious. This conception of the dependent and vulnerable child in need of maternal protection guided by expert insights into the needs of children originated in a concern for the future of the state, which itself arose with the modern 'gardening' attitude to government. If we follow Donzelot (1979) then, the 'dependent child', the human becoming in need of careful tending, is a product of the formation of modern states. The knowledges and practices aimed at controlling children's development are central to the process of modernization. Children's special status as sites of investment meant that they needed to be regulated and closely supervised, not only for their own sake, but also for reasons of state. The results of this identification of children as dependent becomings, whose dependence depends on the state, are all around us today. As Rose (1989) puts it:

Childhood is the most intensively governed sector of personal existence. In different ways, at different times, and by many different routes varying from one section of society to another, the health, welfare, and rearing of children has been linked in thought and practice to the destiny of the nation and the responsibilities of the State. The modern child has become the focus of innumerable projects that purport to safeguard it from physical, sexual and moral danger, to ensure its normal development, to actively promote certain capacities of attributes such as intelligence, educability and emotional stability.

(Rose 1989: 121)

Child concern: from reasons of state to the interests of the child

So far, we have seen how children became identified as dependent becomings just as the model of the developmental state emerged. We have argued that the understanding of children as totally and necessarily dependent was *itself* dependent on the adoption of the model of the developmental state. It was the preservation of children for reasons of state that made childhood seem so thoroughly dependent. In short, without the model of the developmental state, childhood would not today be identified as a period of total and necessary dependency. But, as we shall now see, the connection that has been established between childhood and dependency is currently providing children with a certain sort of *independence*. Through the UN Convention (see www.un.org) children's dependency is becoming a basic principle of global regulation. They are being provided with an identity outside the concerns and reasons of single states. In the age of uncertainty, children are becoming objects of concern in their own right. To address this issue we need to spend some time examining the shifting grounds of concern, feeling and consideration for children as dependants.

One feature of the being/becoming division that has been rather muted in our account so far is the close relation between children's dependency and adults' emotional responses to them. In stark contrast to Donzelot's (1979) campaigners for the preservation of children, present-day campaigns around childhood are less likely to refer directly to reasons of state, and more likely to refer to the needs and interests of the *child*. As Stainton Rogers and Stainton Rogers (1992) have argued, agendas of child concern can change over time. While in the eighteenth century, Chamousset could quite happily envision training children for military combat, his contemporary counterparts are more likely to try to move us to action *against* such uses of children. See, for example, the website of the organization 'Warchild' (www.warchild.org). The child who is the focus of concern for their own sake is no longer the child as future state citizen, but the child as global citizen in the present. It is precisely the figure of the child set inappropriately to adult tasks, the dependant betrayed by adults, the dependant whose interests are not respected by adults in power and authority, that can offend us when considering child soldiers, child labourers or child prostitution. This sensitivity to the betrayal of children, wherever in the world they may be, is certainly a sign of the successful spread of the notion of childhood dependency from its origins in European states. But, as we shall see, it is also an indication of a relatively recent 'decoupling' of children's interests from reasons of state.

Unlike the majority of Donzelot's (1979) sources, we have become used to being emotionally and morally *moved* by adults' failure to respect children's special status as growing dependants. To some extent, Donzelot's (1979) arguments might have predicted this. Just as states and parents took on *rights* to preserve children, they also took on the duty and responsibility so to do. But while we may still believe in the right and duty of states to ensure that children are adequately educated and preserved as future economic forces, we are also able to see children's interests in distinction from, even in contrast to, the plans and concerns of national governments. We no longer see children solely as the property of the adult 'gardening' state. We also see them as worthy of concern in their own right and deserving of attention for their own sake. Donzelot's (1979) historical work can scarcely be expected to offer an account of how this might have come about. One question remains for us, then, in our account of childhood and dependency: how have the interests of the dependent child come to be separated from reasons of state?

There are accounts of the history of childhood that do pay attention to the focusing of emotional and moral investment and concern on children for their own sake. Ariès (1962) argued that before the sixteenth century, there was no conception of childhood as a period of life distinct from adulthood. He argues that the categorical division 'adult/child' was simply not available. As he charts the development of this distinction in the lives of wealthy Europeans and its spread throughout society, he draws our attention to the emergence of the 'coddling' of children. This 'coddling' will be familiar to many contemporary readers. It consists of a delighted celebration of examples of children's clumsiness, incompetence and general confusion at the world. The less capable in the management of their bodies and the less subtle their handling of social relationships, the greater the love and attention given them. Thus, as the category 'childhood' spread, so individual children could be celebrated for their childishness. Turning from private emotional sentiments to the public expression of moral sentiments, Hopkins (1994: 3) identifies the 'growth of humanitarianism in the second half of the eighteenth century' as a key factor in forming the attitudes of nineteenth-century English social reformers. It seems that policies designed to improve working-class children's lives, bringing about the gradual reduction of child labour over the nineteenth century, were as much influenced by sentiments of horror at cruelty and exploitation as they were by the perceived need to preserve children from the workplace for the purposes of education.

Nevertheless, we are left with little understanding of how a perception of children as especially weak and vulnerable can now be taken as a pillar of international regulation, cropping up as it does in the UN Convention on the Rights of the Child. The Convention exists partly to specify the limits of state ownership of children, to distinguish between reasons of state and the interests of children who live under them. It achieves this by allowing that children should have some ownership of themselves. For example, Article 3 provides that:

> In all actions concerning children, whether undertaken by public or private social welfare institutions, courts of law, administrative authorities or legislative bodies, the best interests of the child shall be a primary consideration.
>
> (General Assembly of the UN 1989)

The Convention makes children objects of concern in their own right, outwith the plans and interests of national governments, under the gaze of global regulation. So by the beginning of the twenty-first century, the dependent child is still closely tied by history and national policies to the furtherance of state ambitions, but is also, by virtue of their dependence, afforded at the very least a notional degree of *independence* from the state. Children count in their own right as dependent persons. They have their own interests that can be quite different from those of their government. As we shall now argue, this recent development in the shape of child concern is closely tied to a relative decline in the powers of states, a decline in their ability successfully to lay claim to ownership of their populations and in their ability to control the lives of their citizens.

Globalization and dependency

We have already had a taste of what the term 'globalization' means. In Chapter 1 we saw how international economic events of the 1970s were able to shatter the relatively stable socio-economic relations that had been carefully built within many states between 1945 and the early 1970s. To speak of a 'new economy' (Arthur *et al.* 1999), then, is to speak of a situation in which the ability of states to ensure their economic stability by balancing their internal levels of production and consumption is much diminished. The growing economic interdependence of states tends to decrease the strength of national boundaries (Castells 1997). Much of the present-day flow of capital, for example, takes place beyond the control of national governments in international dealing in shares, futures, derivatives and currencies (Castells 1997: 245). When governments begin to lose the power to regulate their domestic economies, to set wage levels, for example, or to balance production and consumption, even the short to medium-term future of the state becomes uncertain. It becomes difficult to know how to colonize this uncertain future, to predict what sort of person is best suited to that future. Further, there are few guarantees that investments made in the young will produce a reliable return. However carefully preserved they are, children may grow into an adulthood of permanent unemployment; they may become economic migrants, seeking opportunity in other wealthier countries; or, if they have the good fortune to become prosperous as adults, the bulk of their expenditure may go on imported goods, returning little on the state's investment.

There is, then, a marked contrast between contemporary conditions and those in which the developmental state emerged. The rulers of Bauman's (1987) 'gardening' states could act as gardeners because their state had clear boundaries that could be preserved and guarded, allowing for the control of all that lay within. The child-rearing experts and hygienists of family life that populate Donzelot's (1979) accounts also relied on this boundary. The boundedness of their state and the distinctiveness of their population formed a firm basis for the rhetoric of national progress that infused the preservation of children. But today, the conditions that once brought faith in the future, faith in authorities' ability to mould that future and, thus, the reasons and legitimacy behind a simple equation of childhood and dependency, are no longer in place. As the future becomes uncertain, as the *dependency* of states themselves becomes clear across the globe, the close links between reasons of state and childhood dependency are being disrupted. To say that the links between states and their children have been entirely broken would be a gross exaggeration. Nevertheless, as we have seen, the difference between reasons of state and the interests of the child are now recognized in international regulation. Currently, then, the global child citizen is positioned in overlapping states of dependence and independence. As global citizens, children have interests of their own that may be different from those of their state, whether or not their state recognizes those interests. Children may still be seen as dependent, but they are no longer dependent on states for that dependence. In the age of uncertainty, children can be considered in independence of state government for the first time.

Conclusion: dependency and ambiguity

In this chapter, we have tried to account for the widespread identification of childhood with total and necessary dependency. The most important argument we have developed is that the equation of childhood with dependency lies in the history of nation-states and in the widespread adoption of the developmental state model. Seen as investments for the future of the state, children had to be protected from any contamination that might reduce the return on the investment. This meant separating children from wider society and exerting tight control over any of their contacts that could not be eliminated. So it was 'wise' investment in human resources that made children seem totally and necessarily dependent. Our argument is that children became seen as peculiarly weak and vulnerable *because* they were treated as investments that might be damaged. Within the developmental state model, children's interests were no different from those of the state. Child experts and parents (mothers in particular) could 'borrow' legitimate authority over children's lives by playing a part in the developmental state.

But this chapter also had a second theme, that of the growing ambiguity of the state of childhood dependence. Children were isolated and preserved within the developmental state. Their dependency was at once a result of and a justification for this preservation. But as the dependency of states themselves is being revealed through economic globalization, childhood's dependency is providing children with an identity *outside* the state, an identity as global citizens. Even though the figure of the global child citizen is principally defined through weakness and vulnerability, it is by virtue of their dependency that they can now be considered in independence of reasons of state. In the age of uncertainty, as a global economy and global forms of regulation emerge, childhood dependency is becoming a source of ambiguity in the relationship between children and states. Children's dependency can no longer guarantee adult authority over children.

3

Beings in their own right?
The recognition and
mis-recognition of children

Over the course of Chapters 1 and 2, we have tried to account for the widespread credibility of the being/becoming division. We have tried to explain why it seems to make such good sense to divide 'humans' into adult 'human beings' and child 'human becomings'. In Chapter 2 we accounted for the emergence of the category 'human becoming'. We charted a connection between the development of the modern state and the understanding and treatment of the young as embodiments of the future. As the young became the focus of investment, so it came to seem appropriate and legitimate to attempt to control and manage their lives and experiences, so that they would become useful as adults. The link that was forged in the eighteenth and nineteenth centuries between the fate of the state and the nature of children's living conditions underlay the production of the category 'human becoming'. So, if we now live in a world in which the adult/ child distinction is widely used and seems to make good sense, then this is partly because childhood, understood as a period of 'becoming', has been a fundamental element of states' government and use of their populations. Turning to the 'being' side of the distinction, we saw in Chapter 1 how mid-twentieth-century socio-economic conditions and organizing principles of work and intimate life helped to produce an image of 'standard adulthood'. As many adults came to live with confident knowledge of their place in society, definitions of adulthood as stable completion became clear enough to be contrasted with childhood's incomplete becoming.

So the account we have offered of the widespread use and apparent good sense of the human being/human becoming distinction is as follows: in the twentieth century, views of children as unstable, changeable embodiments of the future met socio-economic conditions in which adulthood could be understood as a condition of stability. This conjunction maximized the contrast between adult and child and made them look like different types of human. Wherever governments treated children as embodiments of the future, and wherever socio-economic conditions allowed adulthood to be lived as stability, the idea that humans could and should be divided into human beings and human becomings became almost unquestionable. Clearly these conditions were not met everywhere in the world. But they were met in a sufficient number of powerful and influential countries to allow for the distinction to make its mark on the current pattern of global regulation of the meanings of 'humanity' in UN conventions and declarations.

Why have we spent so much time trying to account for the salience of the adult/child distinction? We have noted that the distinction has become 'almost' unquestionable. We have also noted that the distinction has been of great significance in giving adults power and authority over children. But what if adults' authority over children was not always legitimate? What if adults' power over children made some children vulnerable to exploitation? If adults make decisions for children, is it possible that they sometimes make bad decisions? By trying to explain why it *seems* to make such good sense to think about adults and children as different types of humans rather than just accepting that it does makes good sense, we have put ourselves in a position to ask whether it *still* makes good sense for us to divide humans into two types according to age. Having some idea of where the distinction comes from, we are now able to choose whether to endorse it or not.

We have suggested that the adult/child distinction became 'almost' unquestionable in the mid-twentieth century. But since the early 1990s, a set of approaches to the sociological study of childhood emerged that were based on a critical attitude toward the adult/child distinction. These approaches are based on the view, which we have already advanced, that since the adult/child distinction is a product of history and changing social relations, it may not always be a reliable guide to our thinking. In this chapter we shall see how sociologies of childhood have developed alternative approaches to studying relationships between adults and children that offer new ways of making judgements and decisions about them. We shall chart the areas on which this diverse set of approaches agree – principally their opposition to a 'dominant framework' (James and Prout 1997: 10) of understandings of children and childhood – and some of those on which they differ. By the end of the chapter it should be clear why these approaches share the view that children should be understood as 'beings' in parity with adults. But we shall also spend some time thinking about whether the sociologies of childhood, in their present form, are an adequate response to the conditions of the age of uncertainty. The main issue here is whether it makes sense to see children as 'beings' when 'standard adulthood', our main model of human 'being', is losing its socio-economic supports. In a return to the themes of the latter part of Chapter 1, we shall ask whether, in an era of flexible adulthood in which flexibility is the medium of adult life, 'being' is a good word for adulthood or for childhood.

We shall begin our survey of the sociology of childhood with an examination of its critique of those knowledges of children that are based on the powerful ideas of socialization and development.

What is the 'dominant framework'?

What does it mean to think of children as human becomings? It certainly means thinking of them as travellers on a journey toward adulthood, the state that we have seen defined and lived as 'stable' during the twentieth century. But in the 'dominant framework' (James and Prout 1997: 10) that the sociology of childhood criticizes, children's journey has been understood not just as a journey toward adulthood, but also, and more fundamentally, as a journey toward being *fully human*. As we shall see, it is the distance that the dominant framework places between children and full humanity that sociologists of childhood find most objectionable. Their argument is that the dominant framework of knowledge about children makes us fail to recognize them as fully human.

We shall build our picture of the dominant framework by examining two influential theories about 'growing up'. These theories tend to work from the assumption that children are in some sense incomplete, that they are not *fully* human. Though children are of the same biological species as adults, *full* humanness is never just a matter of biological classification; 'nature' is never enough. Whether in psychological or sociological accounts of growing up, children have been seen as starting their journey close to nature and gradually moving away from it, becoming more like human beings as they grow either more 'rational' or more 'cultural'. Biologically grounded propensities to learn and to think about the world may help children along the way; indeed it is difficult to imagine children growing up without some physiological capacity to sense the world around them, but the path of becoming is the path toward transcending the state of being just a biologically classifiable physical body.

The journey toward completeness has been depicted in two main ways, each of which carries a particular view of what *supplements* a physical human body needs in order to qualify as a human being. Though both sociology and psychology have shared a view of childhood as a journey toward completeness, they have differed over what children are lacking. The predominant sociological view tends to highlight children's lack of mental *contents* (cultural values and conventions) while the predominant psychological view tends to highlight children's inability, relative to adults, to undertake certain mental *processes* that amount to 'rationality'.

Socialization and conventions

There is reason to believe that among the learned elements of personality, in certain respects the stablest and most enduring are the major value-orientation patterns and there is much evidence that these are 'laid down' in childhood and are not on a large scale subject to drastic alteration during adult life.

(Parsons 1951: 101)

Sociology has long sought to describe the transition from human becoming to human being in terms of 'socialization'. Socialization has been described by the influential sociologist Talcott Parsons as 'the internalization of the culture of the society into which the child is born' (Parsons 1956: 17). On Parsons' account, when children are born they are unaware of the conventional moral values with which fully fledged members of the culture make judgements about right and wrong; they are ignorant of the expectations that define normal or appropriate conduct within that culture; and they have no notion of the duties and responsibilities that members of the culture believe they have toward one another. In short, children are born in ignorance of social conventions. As children grow they are gradually informed about those social conventions. They receive instruction from their parents and other adults about the 'patterns of value' (Parsons 1956: 17) that they should uphold and live by in order to qualify as a cultural member. As this process of learning or 'internalization' proceeds, the child's emptiness is filled with the knowledge they need to understand the conduct of others, to be comprehensible to others and, ultimately, to be recognized by others, through mutual comprehension, as a fully fledged member of its culture. Without this cultural supplementation, without taking part-ownership of shared values, a person could never live a fully human life, since for Parsons, a fully human life involves the ability to make sense of, and make sense to, other cultural members.

It is clear that different cultures will teach children different conventions but, whatever the society or culture in question, on Parsons' account some process of socialization or other is vital, both for each child and for the society in general. The means by which children are instructed may differ. Internalization may or may not be encouraged, for example, by physical punishment. Likewise, it may or may not be dramatized in special rites of passage. But without adequate socialization, children will suffer in later life because they will never find their place in society. Socialization is as important for the society as a whole as it is for the individual person. Unless children are adequately socialized, the culture or society in question will be unable to reproduce itself as a structure of mutual comprehension and agreed convention and it will fall into disorder.

On Parsons' view then, socialization is not only something that just takes place, but also something desirable. The child undergoing this important process of socialization experiences a decrease in ignorance, a decrease in unawareness and gradually becomes more sure of their place in the social world through a firmer grip on convention. Adulthood and full humanity is the achievement of independence, confidence and certainty through the acquisition of knowledge of one's place in society. Once a set of values belongs to the growing person, they belong to their society. Socialization, as Parsons envisaged it, is a process that rescues each child from the incompleteness of 'nature', and thereby rescues each society from the disorder and decay that would result if its population were incomplete. In short, children are human becomings and must be recognized and treated as such lest they remain incomplete and a threat to society as a whole. As our opening quotation made quite clear, for Parsons, socialization is the passage to adult stability.

Parsons has been criticized for overemphasizing the degree to which societies have a consensus over values, norms and conventions, and for overemphasizing society's ability to determine the values and norms that children internalize. There has been lively debate in sociology about the value of Parsons' picture of socialization. For Wrong (1961), Parsons has an 'over-socialized' conception of what it is to be fully human. Indeed, it is difficult to see how Parsons' account allows for the possibility of cultural and social change. From our own perspective, we can certainly see how closely Parsons' views mirror the picture of adulthood as a period of stability within a generally stable society that was prevalent in his time. The developmental state's view of childhood as a site of investment for the future of society is echoed in, and reinforced by, Parsons' placement of socialization at the heart of society.

Development and rationality

Parsons' sociological view of childhood treated cultural values and conventions as the supplement to nature that was necessary to complete children as fully human. One became an adult by learning to belong to a specific society. The possession of specific mental contents allowed one human 'being' and a role in the reproduction of the social order one belongs to. In Piaget's (1955) very influential cognitive-developmental theory of growing up it is not so much the presence or absence of mental contents that separates human becomings from human beings, as the way that they process information about the world. Children and adults differ in the extent to which their reasoning about the world is both self-consistent and consistent with the structure of the physical world. For Piaget (1955) these two forms of consistency amount to 'rationality'.

The path to rationality leads away from 'egocentrism' (Piaget 1955: xii) and away from the perception of the world as a jumble of unconnected sense experiences. For Piaget, infants are 'egocentric' because they are unable to make any discrimination between the world and themselves. Infants mistake parts of the world beyond their body for parts of themselves. This egocentrism continues to haunt the child's thinking about the world until full development, taking various forms at different stages of development. Piaget (1955: 229) interprets some young children's conduct, for example, as rooted in a 'magico-phenomenalistic' understanding of causality. Because they are unable fully to distinguish between themselves and the rest of the world, to recognize, say, their feet as belonging to them in a way that another object, such as a chair, does not, their ability to move their feet at will leads them mistakenly to imagine that they are capable of moving any object at will. It is only as their experience of the real nature of the world grows, and they make comparisons between their different experiences, that children are able to draw more realistic conclusions about their causal efficacy. So one important feature of cognitive development is the child's growing ability to take possession and control of themselves and to know the limits of their possession and control by distinguishing between themselves and the rest of the world.

If the developing child grows to see themselves as a physical unity separate from the rest of the world, so they also grow to see the world outside themselves as unified by consistent logical relationships, rather than as a series of unconnected sense experiences. The growing child must rise to the challenge of understanding that the physical world is governed by consistent laws. Here is one of Piaget's examples of children's failure so to do:

> By following the course of immediate experience the child begins by believing that small boats float because they are light; but when he sees a tiny piece of lead or a little pebble gliding along at the bottom of the water, he adds that these bodies are doubtless too light and small to be held back by the water; moreover, big boats float because they are heavy and can thus carry themselves.
>
> (Piaget 1955: 382)

For Piaget the problem this child has is an over-reliance on 'immediate experiences' of heaviness and lightness, and a failure to look behind those experiences for deeper explanatory principles of floating boats and sinking pebbles. Even though the child is able to offer explanations of physical events, he does not notice that these explanations are mutually contradictory, that in some cases he is claiming that it is lightness that allows for floating, while in others he is claiming that heaviness does the job; 'if one remains on the surface of things, explanation is possible only at the price of continuous contradictions' (Piaget 1955: 382).

The physical world presents itself to the senses as ever-changing and inconsistent; both little and big boats can float. The fully developed adult, however, is able to recognize a 'coherent system of totality' (Piaget 1955: 383) behind these fleeting experiences. Though we are born with the physical ability to perceive 'immediate experiences', this ability alone is not sufficient. To become human beings we must learn to mistrust appearances, to separate ourselves from the world, to transcend our incomplete natures. This requires effort on the part of the growing child, who is an active participant in their own development, setting contradictory appearances against each other and searching for unifying principles. The rational human being is not swayed or confused by the complexity of the world, but, by having distance from immediate experience, is able to accommodate their patterns of thought to the real, consistent nature of the physical world. Development is a journey away from disorder and failure to discriminate between self and world, toward order and discrimination, a 'transition from chaos to cosmos' (Piaget 1955: xiii).

Where Parsons (1951) had the growing child supplemented by an accommodation to the regularities of value and consistent expectations of a particular social world, Piaget (1955) has the growing child supplemented by an accommodation to self-consistent and reliable regularities of the physical world. In both cases the child travels from disorder, instability and confusion to order, stability and confidence by transcending their mere biologically classifiable human body. In both cases the process of supplementation allows the child to come into possession of and control over themselves.

The dominant framework: a summary

Though Parsons (1951) and Piaget (1955) differed over what supplements a child would need in order to become fully human, viewed from the critical perspective of sociologies of childhood, their work has much in common. As we now outline the points on which they agree, we shall be unfolding the main features of what James and Prout (1997) call the 'dominant framework'.

The first point to notice is that both Parsons (1951) and Piaget (1955) are offering solutions to the deep philosophical question of what it is to be human. Their answers however are neither of a purely speculative nor of a purely factual kind. As Parsons and Piaget depart from mere biological classification in their description of humanness, they each develop 'prescriptions' for humanness. Each theory gives us a picture of what normal growing up is or should be like. In each case, growing up is a movement away from dependency, and the path away from dependency leads to individual confidence in one's possession of either a particular knowledge base or general thinking skills. For Parsons (1951) that knowledge is clearly of a conventional kind, the values varying between cultures, while for Piaget (1955) there is one universal gold standard of rational thought. Both theories tell us how human order and stability, either on an individual level of consistency of thought or on a social level of integration and coordination, are rescued from nature's inadequacy, how in other words, we come to be self-possessed. Within this framework, human beings, regardless of their place in history or culture, have been faced with the same problem of the maintenance of personal and social order and must tackle this problem by ensuring that they treat their children as becomings. If children are either not socialized properly or encouraged to develop rationality, the result of their incompleteness will be disorder, instability or inconsistency on an individual or social scale.

The dominant framework, then, endorses the treatment of children as special case of humanity. It portrays children as peculiarly malleable and ties this malleability to an incompleteness that stems from their proximity to 'nature' and their lack of self-possession. Not only are particular strategies of completion endorsed by the dominant framework, but also these strategies are set within a universal human drama of the struggle for order. The dominant framework, then, takes the view that children are, first and foremost, sites of investment. Within the terms of the human drama they can be nothing else. Within the dominant paradigm then, it is only right and proper to recognize and to treat children as human becomings rather than human beings because, first of all it is simply the case that they are becomings, and second, because that is the way to give the desired shape and order to future adults and to future society. Now that we have spent some time describing the dominant framework, we are in a position to chart James and Prout's (1997) response to it, and to see how this response deals with the human being/human becoming issue.

Challenging the dominant framework

James and Prout's (1997) critique of the dominant framework is primarily concerned with issues of the recognition and mis-recognition of children. Stated simply, their argument is that the dominant framework leads us to see children in stereotyped terms and that, if we always try to understand childhood through it, then we may simply fail to notice situations in which it is misleading. To be accurate in our studies of children, and fair in our treatment of them, we must abandon our stereotype of them, and try to recognize them for what they are – persons in their own right. The mis-recognition of children is a complicated matter. It hinges on the 'universalism' of the dominant framework, that is to say on its ability to pass itself off as a complete account of childhood and thus to exclude other accounts from our consideration. We shall outline James and Prout's (1997) critique through a close examination of that 'drama' of the human struggle for order.

As we have seen, both Parsons (1951) and Piaget (1955) wove children into a universal human drama of the struggle for order. Whether the goal of this struggle is taken to be the order of rational thought, in which there is a harmony between the reality of the world and the structure of our thinking, or the order of cultural values, in which conventions are shared or at least understood by all, all children, wherever they are located historically or culturally, play much the same role. Rather than playing individual persons, each with his or her own desires and motivations, they play *the* child. *The* child is struggling to transcend the natural order of ignorance of culture or of the fleeting impressions of immediate experience, an order that, in itself, is never quite enough to qualify children as fully human. *The* child is dependent on the assistance of those other characters who have achieved orderly transcendence through culture or rationality – adults. These others should be forgiving of the mistakes the child makes (for they will be many) and generous with the assistance they offer the child, because their future security depends on each and every child's successful and orderly completion.

This drama has all the features of what has been called a 'grand narrative' (Lyotard 1984), a story that is so broad in scope and ambition, and so clear about the responsibilities and powers of the characters it describes, that it can persuade us that it has taken *everything* into account. Not only does the drama promise us a complete account, but also it gives us reasons to try to treat children well, to be morally good as adults. It has many positive features, encouraging, for example, a caring and forgiving attitude to the young. The trouble is that this drama so persuasively promises to encompass all possibilities and so persuasively speaks for the good, that it can lead us to forget the *exclusions* it performs. It gives a clear picture of how adults should relate to children because it gives a clear picture of what children are. But in doing so it excludes the possibility of recognizing children as individual persons. Whatever its positive features, the dominant framework hides actual children behind the figure of the universal child. As James and Prout (1997: 11) put it, within the dominant framework 'children do not have to appear . . . the child . . . can represent all children'.

The dominant framework carries a particular way of interpreting the things actual children do and say. As long as children can be seen, in the terms of the drama, as irrational, or as ignorant of the nature of the society in which they live, then the things they do and say can be interpreted as reflections of their limitations rather than as expressions of their own intentions, desires or opinions. Likewise when they are identified with *the* child, children's interactions with adults can be seen as steps along the journey toward the future state of completion rather than as encounters between people that have effects on and consequences for them both in the here and now. In the dominant framework children are not social actors, but are merely recipients of supplementation.

For James and Prout (1997) *the* child of the dominant framework is problematic because it stands between us and actual children. It makes us interpret each child as if it were *the* child with all its limitations and inadequacies, and thereby stops us from noticing situations in which children depart from the stereotype. For example, if a given child did have intentions, desires and opinions of their own, the dominant framework would not recognize them. Being at odds with a parent over some issue would indicate a need for further socialization rather than a genuine and well-grounded disagreement. At best a child's claim to have intentions, desires and opinions of their own would be overshadowed by their incomplete self-possession and self-comprehension, and thus taken with a grain of salt. In other words, the dominant framework has the power to 'mute' children, to render them silent and invisible, heard and seen not for themselves but for their resemblance to a character in a narrative of maturation. Just as it mutes children, the dominant framework grants adults the position of legitimate authorities over them, capable of knowing better than them and speaking more fully on their behalf than they are able to.

The effects of the dominant framework are not limited to the interpretation of individual children's speech and actions. Because of its claims to universality, the dominant framework can race ahead of alternative visions of childhood wherever they are offered. Here are a few examples of the speed with which the dominant framework can close down such alternatives. Let's say an account of childhood is offered which makes the case that they should be understood as a *political minority*, excluded from society's decision-making processes much in the same way that women have been in the past. Such a case has been made (Alanen 1994). The dominant account stands ready to rebut this case. With the help of the dominant framework, an argument can be assembled quite quickly that children lack the mental contents and/or mental competences to be involved in making important decisions. It might then be added that those calling for children's enfranchisement by thinking politically about them are failing to show the degree of responsibility toward children that befits adults. Imagine that a history of the place of young people in society is written that shows that they have not always been marked out as becomings and treated differently from adults. At least one history of this kind has been written (Ariès 1962). The dominant framework might allow that those arrangements existed, but, by comparing those arrangements with the drama of the human struggle for order, would swiftly judge the past not just as different from the present, but also as inferior to the present.

The dominant framework as a 'truth regime'

We have now described some of the features and powers of the dominant framework and seen how it can narrow our vision of childhood. The dominant framework 'dominates' by ensuring that any accounts of childhood that differ from it, including those coming from children themselves, can be muted. But what of its scope? Are James and Prout (1997) suggesting that children in *all* circumstances are mistaken for *the child*? Are children always silenced and mis-recognized? To read James and Prout (1997) this way would be to ignore a vital part of their critique.

The degree of influence that the dominant framework has on the pattern of relationships between adults and children varies between different situations. It is at its most influential when adults have to act as *experts* on children and childhood. Experts have to assure themselves and others that their actions and decisions are based on an understanding of the *true* nature of childhood. In a good deal of daily life, the question of whether we are acting on the basis of a true understanding of childhood simply does not arise. Adults can and do meet and interact with children as social actors and as persons in their own right with their own desires, opinions and motives. But there are many circumstances in which actions toward and decisions about children do have to meet the requirement of being based on *truth*, on firm understandings of what children in general are like and of what they need. These are circumstances marked by controversy and differences of opinion among adults, situations where knowledge and power are closely aligned. James and Prout (1997: 23) use social workers and teachers as examples of such expert adults who have to justify their actions to themselves and to others who might disagree with them. The dominant framework tends to be deployed wherever a single authoritative version of childhood is required.

As we saw above, within the terms of the human struggle for order, adults are those who have achieved orderly self-possession, while children are those who have not. So not only do theories of socialization and development provide some of the details of what supplements children are in need of, but also they allow adults to feel confident in their actions and thinking, confident that they know best. The dominant framework is not just a set of dry verbal claims about children and adults, it is rather a 'regime of truth' (Foucault 1977) that we live within and derive our most basic feelings of right and wrong from. The claims that the dominant framework makes are brought to life by their connections with the responsibilities that expert adults face when making decisions about children. Adult anxieties about their ability to make good decisions and to discharge their responsibilities toward children properly can be soothed by the position of complete and self-possessed being that the dominant framework offers them. In effect, the dominant framework acts as a supplement to adults in authority, confirming their completeness, competence and ability to make good judgements whenever it might come into question. It lets adults mistake themselves for *the* adult, the 'standard adult' of Chapter 1. Both the authority of the expert over the child and the self-confidence of the expert, then, are dependent on the application of the dominant framework. Unfortunately the price for this comforting truth regime can be paid by children when they are seen as nothing but examples of *the* incomplete, irrational or ignorant child.

Recognizing children

The dominant framework is persuasive in its ability to give order and meaning to relationships between adults and children; it is useful to those who are involved in deciding what to make of children; and, as a supplement used in times of controversy, it is comforting to adults, especially when they are acting as experts. But at the same time the dominant framework turns children and adults into quite distinct types of human being; denies the possibility of any other view of the adult/child relation; and makes it very hard to see children for what they are, if what they are is any different from *the* irrational, ignorant child. Above all it tends to reinforce the power and authority that adults can exert over children. Now that we have outlined James and Prout's (1997) critique of the knowledges surrounding children, we can turn to their alternative vision of children and childhood research.

Academic theories and research, such as the work of Parsons (1951) and Piaget (1955), have been a crucial relay in the legitimation of adult authority over children. For James and Prout (1997) the best place to start questioning that authority is with the formation of new knowledges about children. Where children have been muted and made invisible, where children have been mistaken for *the* child, James and Prout (1997) want to hear their voices and see them for what they really are – social agents in their own right. To this end, they draw together what they call a new 'emergent paradigm' (James and Prout 1997: 8), a collection of commitments that they hold in common with those other sociologists of childhood who share their feelings about the dominant framework. Each of these commitments contradicts one or other aspect of the dominant framework. Rather than see children in relation to nature, the new paradigm would see childhood as a social phenomenon, as a social institution that is the result of historical, political and economic processes. We gave a version of this view in Chapter 2. Rather than think in terms of *the* child, a diversity of *childhoods* should be recognized, since children's experiences vary with their ethnicity, social class and gender. Rather than study children so as to give answers to the very adult questions of how to maintain social order, the new paradigm should be able to study children's social relationships and cultures 'independent of the perspective and concerns of adults' (James and Prout 1997: 8). In sum, the overgeneralized image of the incomplete child who is in need of supplementation, the image of the child as lacking desires, opinions and motives of her own, needs to be replaced. As James and Prout (1997) put it:

> Children are and must be seen as active in the construction and determination of their own social lives, the lives of those around them and of the societies in which they live.
>
> (James and Prout 1997: 8)

The new paradigm is an attempt to study children and childhood in a way that does not always support and confirm adult authority, power and superiority. In order properly to recognize children, researchers must make a firm decision *not* to apply the dominant framework. They must choose to see children as human beings, active participants in social life, rather than as human becomings, passive recipients of socialization. The effect of this alternative approach is to empty out the category 'human becomings', and to make it possible for researchers and theorists to recognize children as beings alongside adults. Where there were two types of humans, the new paradigm sees only one – the human being who is a social agent. Apart from any effects this might have on the way academics theorize, plan and carry out research, because academic work has fed into the constitution of children's lives in the past, James and Prout (1997) are hopeful that the new paradigm will play a part in changing the pattern of relationships between adults and children in society at large. They write that 'to proclaim a new paradigm of childhood sociology is also to engage in and respond to the process of reconstructing childhood in society' (James and Prout 1997: 8).

Varieties of new paradigm research

Now that we have described the dominant framework and indicated some of its limitations, we can describe some of the alternative approaches to the social study of childhood that have been developed in recent years. We shall compare three prevalent approaches to the task of recognizing children in sociological research: recognition through ethnography; recognition through macro-analysis; and recognition through standpoint. Each of these approaches offers an alternative to the universal stereotype of children that the dominant framework offers. They each share the view that the dominant framework generalized about childhood far too much, obscuring variety in the experience of childhood and in the characteristics, capabilities and activities of particular children. Each, then, is a reaction against the tendency to recognize children only as *the* child. Though these approaches share an opposition to the dominant framework, we shall see that they also differ over how best to recognize children as 'human beings' in research practice.

Recognition through ethnography

Ethnography is a particularly useful methodology for the study of childhood. It allows children a more direct voice and participation in the production of sociological data than is usually possible through experimental or survey styles of research.

(James and Prout 1997: 8)

In ethnographic research, the researcher's goal is to understand the *meanings* that social participants apply to one another and to one another's conduct. Ethnography is driven by questions about how people understand their social world and the other people in it; how these understandings are in-fluenced by individuals' social position; and how people understand their social position and actively respond to it. The ethnographic researcher will typically spend a good deal of time observing and participating in the social life of a relatively small group of people. Since ethnography focuses on small numbers of people and pays close attention to how they interact with and understand each other, it is often referred to as working on the 'micro' level. Working at the micro level through conversation and participation means that the ethnographer is close to their research participants. They are in a position to listen to research participants as individuals. Because the ethnographer's primary task is to discover research participants' views of themselves and of each other, ethnographers are also obliged to put their own theories, assumptions and preconceptions of the people and contexts they are researching to one side.

Perhaps the most important feature of ethnography, as a way of recog-nizing children, is that what they say and do during the research period can influence the research agenda of the ethnographer. The questions that the ethnographer becomes curious about tend to emerge from their experi-ences with participants. By contrast, 'experimental and survey styles of research' (James and Prout 1997: 8), to a large extent, require that the researcher decides what aspects of research participants and of their lives are of interest or significance before they conduct their research. Psychological experiments, for example, are carefully designed to supply information to answer just one question. Surveys ask participants to respond to questions that they may not have even thought of before. For James and Prout (1997) this gives them a tendency to obscure children's concerns behind those of adult researchers.

As a strategy for doing research with children then, ethnography does not so much contradict the dominant paradigm as allow for different understandings of the experience of childhood, child–adult relationships and of children's position in society to emerge. It provides opportunities for children's muted voices to be heard and for children as individual social agents to shine through the image of *the* universal child that so often stands in their way. Ethnography, then, recognizes children as individual persons and as social beings. In stark contrast to the 'universalism' of the dominant framework, if generalizations about children and their experiences are to be made from ethnographic data, these will be made on the basis of careful comparison of particular instances, that is to say, after children have had the opportunity to have their say.

Recognition through macro-analysis

'Children as individuals in their own right are virtually absent from many policy discussions' (Huston 1991: 4). If the dominant framework does not allow children to 'count' as fully fledged human beings, then this has had its effects on the way social scientists produce numerical, quantitative data about the social world. When social scientists produce the big or 'macro' picture of society, they often count up who owns what and what services and opportunities they have access to. They go on to interpret these counts in terms of significant variables like ethnicity, socio-economic class and gender. This allows them to develop answers to important questions such as whether life opportunities are influenced by ethnicity, socio-economic class and gender. But, historically, the macro picture of children's lives has been built by assuming that measuring their caregivers' lives tells us all that we need to know. This failure to recognize children in the macro picture has significant consequences when this picture forms the basis of governments' policy decisions.

McLanahan *et al.* (1991) give us an example of this problem in their discussion of a group of social policies designed to tackle poverty in 'mother-only' (McLanahan *et al.* 1991: 74) families in the USA. 'Work-welfare' programmes are designed to enable those single parents who depend on welfare benefits for their income to escape poverty by entering, or returning to, paid employment. Though these programmes vary in their details across the USA, they usually combine a package of training for employment with the provision of inexpensive or free childcare. From adult perspectives, this may look like an ideal solution to the host of problems that many single mothers experience because of their low income. Childcare provision in particular makes single mothers more available for paid employment. But these benefits may be off-set by disadvantages to the children involved. There are no guarantees that the childcare provided will be an adequate replacement for the mother's care. If no one asks what the effects of such policies are on children's lives, no one will know of these possible disadvantages.

For Qvortrup (1997), such problems of the failure of macro-analysis to recognize children has a clear solution; childhood, or rather 'generation', should stand alongside ethnicity, socio-economic class and gender as a key variable of data collection and analysis. This will enable data to be gathered on how changes in employment rates, in family law and in the provision of state welfare impacts on children as a group. Questions of whether and how being a child, rather than an adult, affects one's opportunities and well-being can then be raised and addressed alongside questions of the impact of socio-economic class, ethnicity and gender. Furthermore, interactions between generation and other variables can also be studied, revealing differences in children's lifestyles and opportunities that depend on whether they are girls or boys, in an ethnic minority or majority, and on the status and occupations of their caregiver(s).

Comparing ethnography and macro-analysis

Ethnographic and macro-analytic approaches to the social study of childhood have both been developed as attempts to replace *the* general child of the dominant framework with a fuller recognition of children. In ethnography, *the* child is replaced with actual *children* who are conceived of as individual social participants. In macro-analysis *the* child is replaced with a range of different *childhoods* that are formed as the variable 'generation' overlaps and interacts with other sociological variables. In this way they attempt to replace the dominant framework's stereotype of *the* child either with a recognition of children's diversity as social participants or through a recognition of the variety of childhood as a social category. They both use their own strategies for gathering information to show that not all children are the same. Ethnography listens to individuals and observes small groups of people in interaction. Macro-analysis measures significant features of the living conditions of large numbers of people. The main difference between these approaches, then, is a difference of scale. Ethnography works on a small scale while macro-analysis works on a large scale.

As Qvortrup (2000) indicates, this difference of scale has been the source of some controversy between these two approaches. The controversy can be boiled down to one simple question: which is more important in shaping children's lives and experiences, the other people they meet and interact with face-to-face, or their position in social hierarchies defined by gender, ethnicity, class and generation? This question is about how free we think people are to ignore or change social hierarchies in their daily interactions. There is a tension between recognizing, on the one hand, that people are free to interpret themselves and to treat each other in many different ways, sometimes taking note, for example, of gender, and sometimes not, and, on the other hand, recognizing that factors like class and gender really do shape our lives, sometimes without us realizing. To build a *complete* understanding of childhood that took account both of people's freedom to interpret and of the constraints of social order that are at work 'behind our backs' would require that we finally resolve this tension. Since each side of the tension is firmly built into the ways that ethnography and macro-analysis gather their information, one preferring small-scale conversation, the other preferring large-scale measurement, such a resolution looks unlikely. Our tension is reproduced every time one or other sort of research is undertaken.

So we can see that there is something incomplete and inconsistent about the new paradigm of social research into childhood. Is this worrying? Perhaps not. After all, one of the main problems with the dominant framework was that it could be passed off as complete. That sense of completion is what made it such a comfortable truth regime for adults. Perhaps it is better to approach the social study of childhood through a range of strategies that sometimes agree and sometimes disagree. These issues of resolution and completion bring us to our third example of new paradigm research – recognition through standpoint. We shall see that it tackles our problem of scale by starting off from the view that small-scale interactions between adults and children are thoroughly shaped by large-scale differences between adults and children as social groups, to such an extent that in order properly to recognize children, we would need an entirely new sort of knowledge – knowledge that is developed from children's 'point of view'.

Recognition through standpoint

The 'standpoint' approach is based on a recognition that not everyone is in a position to produce social knowledge. Opportunities to work as a sociologist, to describe society and to give accounts of its rights and wrongs, are distributed by just the same factors that distribute opportunities in other walks of life. For example, just as women are under-represented in the United Kingdom's Parliament, so, historically, women have been under-represented in the ranks of sociology professors. It is even more unusual to find children who are practising sociologists. Does it matter who gets to produce social knowledge? For Smith (1987) and Alanen (1994) it most certainly does.

The 'standpoint' of researchers is made up of their social position and the life experiences that this exposes them to. Researchers' standpoints have an impact on the way they see the social world. Their experiences affect their priorities and their assumptions. Smith (1987) argues that the concerns of mainstream sociology have been profoundly influenced by gender imbalances within the discipline. Mainstream sociology is in fact *'malestream'* sociology. If sociology were dominated by women rather than by men, it would reflect women's experiences and concerns rather than those of men. This much is clear. But Smith (1987) also makes a far more radical argument. Not only would sociology be different if undertaken from a woman's standpoint but also it would be better because it would provide a more complete picture of society. Why does she think this?

For Smith (1987) societies are full of 'ideologies', sets of ideas that make existing social hierarchies, like those between men and women, look inevitable and necessary when, in fact, they are only the result of historical contingencies and are quite open to change. We can see the dominant framework as just such an ideology. The more an ideology makes a social hierarchy seem inevitable, the more those who profit from social hierarchy are likely to believe that ideology. On Smith's (1987) view then, the more powerful a person is, the less likely they are to have an accurate understanding of the nature of society. The standpoint of the powerful yields a mistaken picture of society, while the standpoint of the weak yields a more accurate picture of society. A claim like this is rather controversial, but Smith (1987) supports it with quite a compelling example.

For many years sociology has taken a division between the private sphere of domestic life and intimate relations and public sphere of work and politics for granted. The two spheres were traditionally studied separately from one another. This made sense because from a male standpoint they had been experienced as separate. Thanks to the gendered division of labour, a male sociologist could leave the private sphere behind him as he closed the door of his house on his way to work. According to Smith (1987) women's experience of the relationship between public and private spheres tends to be rather more complicated. Women are far less likely to be able to leave their private lives behind them when they enter the public sphere. Issue of childcare and household labour tend to accompany them into their working lives. For Smith (1987) women's experience is not based on the easy divisibility of the public and the private, but on the struggle to integrate them and to balance their competing demands. So while a male standpoint could see only public and private as fundamentally separate from one another, women's standpoint could see public and private *both* as separable from one another (seeing as men had been able to separate them) *and*, more fundamentally, as inseparable from one another. A women's standpoint, then, would yield a more complete account of relationships between the public and private spheres because it would see those relationships as the result of effort.

Alanen (1994) extends this reasoning about women's standpoint to the case of children. Just as men and women have stood in a hierarchy that limited men's knowledge of the social world in the same moment that it gave them power, so adults and children stand in a hierarchy that limits adults' knowledge of the social world as it gives them power. The dominant framework, with all its limitations, is just one aspect of this. It is through the daily application of the dominant framework to the task of organizing children's lives that the large-scale hierarchy of age and power passes into the small-scale interactions that children are involved in. The dominant framework makes the society-wide difference between childhood and adulthood relevant to every child and every adult, just as ideologies of gender have made large-scale gender hierarchies relevant to every woman and every man. These are the conditions that have allowed the standards of 'standard adulthood' to be applied to children, but to be forgotten in the case of adults. It is from an adult standpoint that children are incomplete and adults complete. We do not yet know what views a child standpoint would yield. This is why Alanen (1994) urges us to develop such a standpoint. It would be a way of recognizing children, just as Smith's (1987) work recognized women.

Standpoint and completion

What would the construction of a child standpoint involve? It would certainly involve the degree of attention to particular children's voices and points of view that ethnography allows us. That would allow us to build a picture of society seen from children's position. A children's standpoint would also need to give an account of 'generation' as a sociological variable. A lot of the theoretical work needed to resolve the tension between these small and large-scale approaches seems to have already been done by Smith (1987). Yet, even though it would seem to solve the new paradigm's major tension, the standpoint approach has not gone without criticism. To recognize children by establishing a child standpoint on the model of Smith's (1987) women's standpoint presents us with an interesting problem. What if children, when asked, gave us a picture of society that was strongly influenced by the dominant framework? Would we then count that as part of children's standpoint, or discount it as ideological? A more general question emerges from this. How could a single standpoint recognize and value the different desires, opinions and motivations of children as separate individuals? James et al. (1998) have seen a repetition of the generalizing and completing tendency of the dominant framework in the standpoint approach. They argue that the standpoint approach repeats the main mistake of the dominant framework – thinking that it is possible and even desirable to transcend the differences between actual children in order to develop a general account of childhood. They call the standpoint strategy into question by arguing that it constitutes 'the imposition of a politicised uniformity that defies the differences within' childhood (James et al. 1998: 31). Just as the tension between large and small-scale analyses is unlikely to be resolved, so this second tension between recognizing children as a group who share a standpoint, and recognizing them as individuals whose views may differ, remains at the heart of the new paradigm. The purpose of highlighting these tensions is not to demonstrate that the new paradigm is fundamentally flawed. Instead the purpose has been to show how debates within the new paradigm have a tendency to keep the question of the recognition of children open and alive where the dominant framework tended to close the question down. Taken as a whole, the different approaches of the new paradigm display a laudable lack of anxiety over their own incompleteness. Taken as a whole, the field of the sociology of childhood is departing from the standards of fixed and complete knowledge and expertise that the image of standard adulthood has demanded of us in the past.

Conclusion: outstanding questions

As it struggles to recognize children, the sociology of childhood is indeed developing new approaches to 'being' adult and 'being' child, approaches that may filter into society's decision-making processes in the future. Later in the book we shall be developing new concepts that may help to intensify this process of development, but for the moment two issues remain outstanding. First, we have seen how the new paradigm seeks to portray children as 'beings'. As standard adulthood is being eroded, however, our traditional view of 'being' as stable completion has begun to look quite inadequate. Is the concept of 'being' as deployed in sociologies of childhood any different from standard adulthood? Second, we have seen how the dominant framework was based on the idea that children needed supplementation, that 'growing up' was a process of increasing supplementation that led to a point of completion. If the new paradigm refuses to see children as incomplete it would seem to have dispensed with the notion of supplementation. This makes it difficult to see how the new paradigm can give us any account of growing up. So has the new paradigm thrown the baby out with the bathwater?

It is difficult to find any examination of 'being' in new paradigm literature that is not based on stability, completion and independence. But the issue has been addressed quite recently in the following few lines:

> this new phenomenon, the 'being' child, can be understood in its own right. It does not have to be approached from an assumed shortfall of competence, reason or significance. The 'being' child is not, however, static, for it too is in time.
>
> (James *et al.* 1998: 207)

From this short statement, it would seem that a rather different concept of 'being' than one based on standard adulthood is implied within the new paradigm. To recognize children as 'beings' is not to pretend that they do not change. But how does the 'being' child change if that change is not to be thought of as the supplementation of a natural lack? What could 'growing up' mean once we have distanced ourselves from the dominant frameworks' accounts of socialization and development. Clearly, the short statement above raises more questions than it answers. We shall return to these outstanding questions in Part three where we shall outline a new understanding of 'becoming' in an attempt to answer these questions.

○ PART TWO

Ambiguities of childhood

○───────────────────────────────────

In Part two we shall survey some of the various 'places' of children in society. Using examples from across the contemporary world and from key periods of history, we shall see that wherever children have been placed in the category 'human becoming' they have also been allotted 'proper' physical places in society. The most common 'proper' places for children have been the family home and the school. We shall see that the categorization of children as becomings and the physical placement of children in their proper places have often been mutually confirming. The more children have been successfully kept in their proper places, the more clearly childhood itself has been seen as a state of human becoming.

We shall also give attention, however, to instances where it has proved difficult to keep children in their proper places and where the proper places they have been given are changing around them. When large numbers of children spend a good deal of time on city streets; when family homes become places of concentrated consumption and choice; and, when schooling turns from books to information and communication technologies, the nature of childhood becomes ambiguous. The studies of city streets, family homes and schools in Chapters 6 and 7 form the basis of an argument that the economic, social and technological changes that are taking place in the age of uncertainty are creating childhoods that do not clearly resemble states of human becoming. New ambiguous childhoods are emerging across the globe.

Chapters 6 and 7 emphasize the importance of the contexts of children's lives in shaping childhood. The more that children live in overlapping or contradictory contexts, the more ambiguous childhood becomes. Chapter 8 takes this theme further, examining deliberate attempts to change the regulatory and legal contexts of childhood. The UN Convention on the Rights of the Child is examined as a promise to provide children with a context beyond their physical location within the boundaries of political states. Recent changes in the position of child witnesses in the criminal courts of England and Wales are examined as an attempt to use video-technology to change space and time around children to help them cope with the pressures and demands of giving testimony in such an 'adult-centred' setting.

By the end of this part it should be clear that, in the age of uncertainty, childhood is being opened to a new set of issues. Once, the most important and basic task in the social study of childhood was to determine whether children were beings or becomings, whether they were in and of themselves deserving of respect and recognition. Such determinations formed the basis both of the dominant framework and the new paradigm of the sociology of childhood. As we have seen, sociologists of childhood have, so far, energetically joined in this effort to resolve childhood's ambiguity and to produce 'closure'. But today, as childhood ambiguity is becoming so widespread, the key issue would not seem to be one of definition and closure, but that of how changing contexts change children's potential for social and economic action and participation. The question of what childhood is *in itself* seems to be fading from relevance just as our traditional notions of being and becoming are eroded.

─────4

Children out of place:
ambiguity and social order

◯─────────────────────────────────────

> To be a child outside adult supervision, visible on city
> centre streets, is to be out of place.
>
> (Connolly and Ennew 1996: 133)

In Chapter 2, we saw how European modernization involved a gradual removal of children from mainstream society into spaces of preservation such as the family home and the school. The developmental state separated children from direct contact with society and, in order to preserve them for the future, ensured that their contact with social life was mediated by adults. It would be easy to imagine that this 'separateness' of childhood was total, and that once a state had become 'modern', children would never go un-accompanied. But childhood's distinctiveness was, and remains, the result of a collection of strategies and cultural mores, more or less successful or widely held, rather than something that has ever been fully achieved. The maintenance of the boundaries between children and the adult world re-quires constant vigilance and action on the part of adults, and the coopera-tion of large numbers of children. To be sure, as an ideal, the protection of the dependant has informed many policies over the years, especially those designed to strengthen the 'nuclear' family, from the design of post-1945 housing stock in the UK (Pickvance 1999), to the state provision of 'family allowances' (Pedersen 1993). But it is important to note that its implemen-tation has taken place at different speeds in different countries and for different social classes. For example, where Donzelot (1979) provides us with examples from eighteenth-century France, Cockburn (1995), cited in James *et al.* (1998), offers a study of late-nineteenth and early-twentieth-century Manchester, a large city in northern England. Between 1850 and 1914 children were gradually removed from the 'public places of the streets and workplace to their homes, schools and organised entertainments'

(Cockburn 1995: 14) through the activities of religious organizations, school authorities and child protection agencies. By 1914 the police had also become involved, seeing it as part of their job to question children seen unaccompanied on the city streets at night. As Cockburn (1995: 14) argues, this increasing control of children's independent movements was partly inspired by a mood 'that was concerned with the training of young citizens into future participation in the electorate and defenders of the Empire'. Further, contemporary means for preserving children from wider society are inflected by social class just as they were in Donzelot's (1979) eighteenth century. The middle-class, western child is likely to experience 'public places' through the windows of their parents' car (Sibley 1995), while public transport and the streets, with all their implications of dangerous exposure to strangers, are increasingly left to the poor.

The notion that children do not belong in public space, however, is a powerful one, and it has followed modernization from western Europe and North America to the countries of the South (Ennew 1995). But not all children can afford the dubious privileges of dependency and constant adult mediation. In this chapter we shall examine the position of some of those children whose way of life does not conform to the standards of the western, modern middle class, those children who find themselves on the streets and, consequently, 'out of place'. Unsupervised children on city streets are not only physically 'out of place', but also misplaced with regard to the model of the developmental state and with regard to the cultural assumptions that accompany that model. Such children have failed to become 'becomings', but, as we shall see, that does not mean they are understood as 'beings'. Rather, to the extent that states aspire to being developmental states, such children *cannot* be recognized as beings. Since these children do not easily fit into either the category 'being' or 'becoming', they are a source of confusion for any who think in terms of those categories. Their ambiguity is profoundly disturbing to adult authority and, in many cases, such children pay a high price for authorities' confusion. Neither 'becomings' nor individual 'beings', these children, as we shall see, are frequently understood as troublesome or malevolent *packs* or *gangs* to be managed or even eliminated collectively.

In the following sections, then, we shall describe how children 'out of place' have emerged as a problem in both the poorer and richer parts of the world. We shall draw connections between the experience of being 'out of place' and recent socio-economic change. We shall also see how these children's ambiguity with regard to the states of 'being' and 'becoming' has shaped the patterns of adult action and policy that surround them. Though children 'out of place' are to be found throughout the cities of the world, the reasons for their occurrence, the nature of their experience and of adults' responses to them differ markedly between the North and the South. Yet, as we shall see, comparisons can still be made. We begin with an account of the socio-economic context in which 'street children' emerged as a phenomenon in the South.

Developing nations, structural adjustment and street children

The enormous differences in wealth and power between the countries of the North and the South has been a constant concern since the mid-twentieth century, coming into prominence as an issue that needed to be tackled as southern nations achieved political independence from their erstwhile colonial 'masters'. There has long been a consensus that for southern populations to see improvement in their living conditions, the South has needed to be 'developed'. Changing agendas for development have been strongly influenced over the years by powerful northern nations, who have retained great influence over southern social and economic policies through international organizations like the United Nations, the International Monetary Fund (IMF) and the World Bank.

According to Snyder and Tadesse (1995), the earliest development strategy, dating from the end of the Second World War, was 'modernization'. This strategy was based on the view that the best way for southern nations to achieve economic success and advantage for their populations was to follow the lead of the developed world, principally Europe and North America, to become industrialized nations on the Fordist model (see Chapter 1). Development through modernization put countries of the South on a path to the high level of internal socio-economic coordination that was widely assumed to provide long-lasting stability. The move toward Fordist production and away from rural subsistence economies transformed towns and cities from marketplaces and administrative centres to centres of production in their own right. Former rural peasants became the urban poor, 'pulled' to the cities by apparent economic opportunity and 'pushed' from the country by landowners seeking the efficiencies of large-scale agribusiness. Modernization required the development of schooling to ensure a literate and trainable population. It also had an impact on the role of the family. As Boserup (1989) puts it,

> economic development is a gradual change from family production to specialised production of goods and services . . . most of the services that family members in subsistence economies provide for each other (including physical protection, health care and education) are taken over by public institutions or specialised private enterprises.
>
> (Boserup 1990: 14)

From a childhood perspective, then, development through modernization tended to promote western childhood and the model of the developmental state, taking children out of informal employment and education by their families and placing them under the supervision of state organizations.

Many southern nations had to borrow money to finance this industrialization and increase in public-sector spending. Modernization, then, put the South heavily in debt to the North. In Chapter 1, we saw how the recession of the 1970s destabilized Fordism in the industrialized world. The stabilities that had seemed to be the apex of national development were now in question. This economic crisis also had its effects on thinking about the development of the South. Once again, northern social and economic experience was taken as the best guide to southern development. Where state-sponsored Fordist production had been seen as the road to economic improvement, it was now identified as a hindrance to development and participation in the global marketplace. Throughout the 1980s, the major creditors of southern nations – such as the IMF and the World Bank – attached certain new conditions to their loans, using financial power to force economic and social change. The resulting 'structural adjustment pro- grammes' (SAPs) obliged southern nations to cut their public sector spend- ing and to replace government regulation of economic relationships with market mechanisms. The northern move toward 'flexibility' was urged on the South. According to Snyder and Tadesse (1995), by lowering expendi- ture on state health and education services, structural adjustment placed a greater burden on African women to provide health care and education for their children. Similarly, Whiteford (1998) gives a detailed account of how SAPs in Cuba and the Dominican Republic increased unemployment, wid- ened the gap between rich and poor and increased the costs of housing and food. SAPs increased socio-economic inequalities in the South and shifted burdens of childcare and education back onto families.

In the course of forty years, then, southern nations had first been encour- aged to develop city-based coordination of state, industry and population to 'catch up' with North America and western Europe, were saddled in the process with large debts, and were then encouraged to reverse this trend toward Fordism by remoulding their economies on more flexible lines, so as to satisfy their creditors that their debts would be repaid. These twists and turns of development policy occurred under the constant shadows of national debt and, often, political instabilities and armed conflict, which were the legacy of earlier struggles for independence. Whatever the rights and wrongs of the changing agendas of global development policy, the result was that in many southern nations an acceptance of the western model of childhood was coupled with an inability to finance the familial and institutional arrangements necessary to realize that model. A tension was set up between desired standards and lived realities. The result was that many southern children could not fit neatly into the 'becoming' category that had come to seem their proper place. Many had to work, beg and, sometimes, steal to support themselves and their families. It is in this socio- economic context of high levels of poverty and low levels of state support that the number of children living and working on the streets of southern cities grew, and that the problem of 'street children' (Connolly and Ennew 1996) came into being.

Street children and the figure of the 'horde'

The police will kill us, for being in the street, for not going home, for not having a family.

(Godoy 1999: 423)

The term 'street children' covers a wide range of children who have quite different ways of life. Baker *et al.* (1996) describe homeless Nepalese children, 9–15-year-old boys, who live on the streets of Kathmandu working as rag-pickers, beggars and casual labourers, while Van Beers (1996) describes children in the Philippines who run market stalls in Manila. Some 'street children' are orphans of war. Some have chosen to live on the streets in preference to abuse and neglect by their families. Others work alongside other family members making a vital contribution to household income. The wide diversity of these ways of life has led some commentators (Connolly and Ennew 1996; Glauser 1997) to question the usefulness of the term 'street children'. Indeed the term has been criticized as embodying a particular western perspective that, ignoring the differences between them, would see such children only as vulnerable 'becomings'. Some would argue that the category 'street children' is itself part of the globalization of western understandings of childhood that has taken place 'first through colonialism and then through the imperialism of international aid' (Ennew 1995: 202). Recent commentators, then, tend to emphasize the degree to which we should see 'street children' as beings rather than as becomings. To this end, Van Beers (1996) writes:

> Working in the streets to many children means earning an income to contribute to the family's survival or to pay for their own schooling. It brings them self-confidence and self-esteem. It also means having some say in the spending of their earnings.
>
> (Van Beers 1996: 196)

So far then, we have seen that the term 'street children' is used to cover a wide range of experiences. We have also seen that debate over the use of the term has centred on our familiar opposition between views of children as human beings and human becomings. But there is a third understanding of street children, one which results from the mismatch between ideals of childhood 'becoming' and the economic realities of the southern city. This understanding bears the marks of the confusion that strikes adults and adult authority when faced with children who do not fit the being/becoming scheme. Rather than being seen as human becomings or as human beings, street children, because of the ambiguity of their cultural position, are open to being characterized as an undiscriminated, disorderly pack or horde. Scheper-Hughes and Hoffman (1998) illustrate this well in their study of Brazilian street children. They begin their account with a quotation from the Brazilian Constitution of 1987, which runs as follows:

> It is the duty of the family, society and the state to assure with absolute priority the rights of children and adolescents to life, health, food, education, leisure, occupational training, culture, dignity, respect, freedom and family and community life, and in addition to protect them from all forms of negligence, discrimination, exploitation, violence, cruelty and oppression.
>
> (Scheper-Hughes and Hoffman 1998: 352)

This Article contains all the commitments and assurances one would expect from a developmental state. Brazilian adults and authorities have the duty to protect Brazilian children, to ensure their well-being and to provide for their 'occupational training'. Yet in 1993,

> Before dawn . . . a car with a small group of off-duty plainclothes police officers drove up to a sidewalk . . . in downtown Rio de Janeiro and opened fire on a group of more than forty street children . . . Eight died – six on the spot and two at a nearby beach where they were taken and killed execution-style.
>
> (Scheper-Hughes and Hoffman 1998: 352)

How could police officers, who had children of their own, and who, presumably, were upholders of the Brazilian Constitution, kill children in this fashion? The puzzle deepens when Scheper-Hughes and Hoffman (1998: 352–3) report that nearly 20 per cent of respondents to an opinion poll of the Brazilian public sided with the police officers concerned, and that there was 'considerable public support for extrajudicial killings by "death squad" vigilantes'. Clues can be found in further details from that opinion poll. Many Brazilian citizens were fed up with street children's 'criminal', 'dirty' and 'disorderly' behaviour.

One of the murderers explained his conduct by saying that the children were dangerous, that they had been known to attack people and that the day before the shootings, some of the children had thrown stones at a police car. Perhaps some of the children were indeed violent and, perhaps, some of them had thrown stones. Nevertheless, the police response was clearly excessive. Would 'stone throwing' normally merit capital punishment? Beyond the excessive nature of the police response, however, it is their lack of discrimination that concerns us here. Rather than try to track down and arrest particular children for particular crimes, the police officers concerned opened fire on a *group* of sleeping children. Apparently then, it did not matter which children died, as long as some children died. It was as if the elimination of *any* of the children was as desirable as the elimination of *particular* children. The murderers, and the section of the population who supported them, understood these street children neither as human beings, nor as human becomings, but as a subhuman pack or horde. They were dealt with as one might deal with an infestation of rats. For the murderers, each child carried the criminality, dirtiness and disorder of the pack as a whole, each carrying the blame for the activities of any other.

There is another pertinent feature of the style in which the murders were conducted. Though the murderers were police officers – agents of the state – they chose to murder under cover of darkness and when they were off-duty. Though the children were shot in a city centre, and the murderers believed themselves to be justified in their actions, the whole episode was surrounded in furtiveness and secrecy. It is as if the police involved thought that their regular commitments to upholding the law, including the Brazilian Constitution, were actually a constraint on their ability to uphold social order. These murders, then, speak of the inability of the Brazilian state to live up to the ideals expressed in its constitution by legitimate and publicly visible means. In a perverse way, the police officers were pursuing the goals of the Constitution by *eliminating* those children for whom it was not working. Not only did each street child carry the burden of blame for others' conduct, but also they carried the burden of Brazilian 'social embarrassment' (Scheper-Hughes and Hoffman 1998: 353) at the mismatch between the ideal of childhood and socio-economic realities. Arguably, the children's vulnerability to attack arose not only through their destitution, but also through their failure to fit either category of humanity, 'being' or 'becoming'.

It is not only Brazilian street children who occupy this dangerously ambiguous cultural position. Wherever the ideal of childhood becoming is met by the failure of institutions to realize it, street children are at risk of becoming a repository of blame and of being seen and treated as a dangerous horde. As Van Beers (1996) writes:

> Children who live and work on the street are the most visible result of the increasing gap between the rich and the poor . . . Yet they are not perceived in this way by the majority of the public or by governments . . . street children are seen by many as a nuisance . . . a public order problem . . . Thus in the eyes of a large proportion of society, including policy makers and implementors, street children 'disrupt the tranquillity, stability and normality of society'.
>
> (Van Beers 1996: 195)

In the following section, we turn our attention to children 'out of place' in the cities of the developed world. As in our account of the 'street children' of the South, we shall see that the destabilization of Fordism in the late twentieth century lies behind their displacement. We shall see that although their living conditions are rather different from those of southern street children, these groups of children occupy a comparable cultural position of ambiguity. They too appear to adults and adult authority as a horde that threatens social order. Although such children do not receive the barbaric treatment that we saw in our Brazilian example, an examination of the recent UK government policy will show that a similar 'ambiguity' informs their treatment. First, however, we need to give an account of their displacement.

Social capital and community

The western European city of the early to mid-twentieth century was a centre of commerce, of industry and of habitation. A constant concern of city planners was to maintain a balance between levels of industrial and commercial demand for workers, and levels of affordable housing stock of a decent quality. Housing issues were a key node, then, in the close coordination of private and public sector concerns under Fordism. The solution to this problem of balance that was adopted across northern Europe in the 1960s and early 1970s was the rapid construction of new urban and suburban estates to house workers and their dependants. Examples of such estates can be found in the high-rise public housing of the English cities of London, Birmingham and Manchester, in Gellerup, a suburb of the Danish city Aarhus (Diken 1998) and in the French 'metropolitan periphery' (Wacquant 1996: 122). The intention was to build low-cost housing that was well supplied with local shops and amenities, places where thriving communities could grow. In the cities of the USA, comparable programmes to build public housing were undertaken, such as Chicago's 'publicly built, low income housing units' (Wacquant 1999: 136). Here, with the stark differences in income between black and white city dwellers, and a long history of ethnic segregation, economic needs for public housing were supplemented by the perceived need to contain ethnic tensions.

It is now generally agreed that this solution to cities' housing problems was far from optimal. With the benefit of hindsight, we can see that the speed with which these estates were built sometimes allowed for poor construction of the housing, and a mismatch between the design of the estates and the lifestyles and aspirations of those who would inhabit them. Even as these strategies were being implemented, they received criticism for turning social divisions of wealth and (particularly in the USA) ethnicity into concrete geographical divisions (Sennett 1971). But our key concern here is with how the form of these estates interacted with the recession of the 1970s and subsequent public policy decisions, so that at the present time, many of the children of those estates have become children 'out of place'.

As the availability of relatively low-skilled jobs declined, and as job security diminished, the great estates became pockets of high unemployment and deprivation. They also concentrated large numbers of children and young people together whose future employability was in doubt. As solutions to the distinctly Fordist problem of housing a highly geographically concentrated workforce, the urban and suburban estates and projects were ill-suited to post-Fordist times that demanded a highly flexible and mobile workforce. Western governments largely responded to recession throughout the 1980s by reducing public spending on welfare payments, unemployment benefits and on the upkeep of public housing, further degrading the life chances and quality of life of estates' residents. Estates and projects became identified with high rates of crime and ill-health. By the 1990s, low levels of public expenditure had become taken for granted by policy-makers, but the question remained of how the condition of the urban and suburban poor could be improved.

Through the late 1980s and early 1990s such concepts as 'community' (Etzioni 1993) and 'social capital' (Coleman 1994) were under development by social thinkers in western Europe and the USA. The term 'social capital' refers to ties of trust (Fukuyama 1995), cooperation and mutual support

(Putnam 1993) between family members, neighbours, community members and institutions of local government. Though, as Morrow (1999) argues, the concept of 'social capital' has never been well defined, since the early days of its development, the argument had been advanced that high levels of 'social capital' were vital for the economic well-being of families, neighbourhoods and states. With the help of these ideas, the problems of estates and projects became reconceptualized by policy-makers as resulting at least as much from the breakdown of community spirit as from the high concentrations of poverty to be found in these areas. The development of social capital came to be seen as a means to stimulate the economic regeneration of poor neighbourhoods. Those living in deprived areas needed to help themselves by first coming to understand themselves as a community with the potential for collective action, and then by acting as communities, determined to better their conditions, in cooperation with local government and state agencies, such as police and health services. The hope was that increased levels of social capital would result in improved levels of employment and health, and decreased levels of crime. But social capital, difficult as it was to define clearly on paper, also referred to personal feelings and qualities of relationship that were hard to measure. It was difficult to see what kinds of interventions and programmes would help build a resource made of feelings of trust and mutual concern. What sort of intervention could help community members come to trust one another and take pride in their neighbourhood?

Social capital and youth

Since the earliest days of the social capital debate, the peer relationships that children of school age have among themselves, in independence of adults, had been seen as a form of social capital. But this form of social capital, it was argued, interfered with educational attainment (Coleman 1961). Children distracted each other from educational goals. The first form of social capital identified was a negative one, which was generated by children outside of and sometimes in opposition to adult agendas. This identification of children as a pool of inappropriate social capital continued through to Portes and Landolt's (1996) analysis of 'inner-city youth gangs' in terms of the social capital they provided for their members (see Morrow 1999). It was this identification of children's *negative* forms of social capital that indicated how to make a start on developing *positive* social capital. The bad social capital of the young was a major obstacle to the development of good social capital for the community. The more that the activities of the young dominated the streets, the less other residents, feeling threatened and harassed, oppressed and depressed by vandalism and street disturbances, were able to take ownership of their neighbourhood. How could community develop when residents were uncomfortable in their own streets? High concentrations of children 'out of place', in the streets without adult supervision, were now taken to be both a symptom and a *cause* of community deprivation and neighbourhood decay. Thus, the collective activities of the children and young people living in the estates and projects came to be a key site of policy intervention.

As we have seen, increases in public expenditure had been removed from western governments' range of strategies for social improvement and re-generation. So, rather than begin community regeneration by directly tack-ling the problem of low income, the focus of concern was turned on children and young people's peer relationships and the activities they were involved in on the streets when outside adult supervision. Gang membership, van-dalism and the range of petty and serious crimes that children and young people sometimes commit were among the most obvious blocks to the development of community spirit. Social capital could be developed only once crime and the fear of crime had been reduced.

Since it was understood that not only actual crime rates, but also levels of *fear* of crime diminished positive social capital, this new way of thinking about the problem of urban deprivation had an interesting in-built dy-namic. While the clearly criminal activities of the young had to be targeted, any activities that could be seen as having the potential to provoke the *fear* of crime would also need to be addressed. Not only the criminal activities of the young, but also, in the UK, any 'antisocial' activities could now be targeted. As we shall see, the potentially 'antisocial' activities of children under 10 years old in the UK may now include simply being on the streets between 9 p.m. and 6 a.m. without adult supervision.

Children and neighbourhood renewal in the UK

In 1998, the UK government's Social Exclusion Unit published *Bringing Britain Together: A National Strategy for Neighbourhood Renewal* (Social Exclusion Unit 1998). This document outlined government strategy for tackling urban deprivation. Its premises and remedies were those of the new 'social capital' agenda. It set out a 'ten to twenty year plan to turn round poor neighbourhoods . . . to . . . empower local communities to shape a better future for themselves' (Social Exclusion Unit 1998: 8). The problems these neighbourhoods faced were linked to high concentrations of poverty and unemployment. They were (and continue to be) places where 'crime, drugs and vandalism are rife' (Social Exclusion Unit 1998: 10). The docu-ment describes an interlinked set of programmes to tackle the full range of these problems 'from anti-social behaviour to lack of access to shops, banks and IT (information technology)' (Social Exclusion Unit 1998: 8).

Bringing Britain Together paid special attention to children and young people, since poorer neighbourhoods tended to have 'more young people, with child densities a fifth higher' (Social Exclusion Unit 1998: 15) than UK average. One of the five themes of the document was 'building a future for young people' (Social Exclusion Unit 1998: 11), which focused on children as 'becomings'. A clear way to build a future for young people was to ensure that they were well equipped for the future through improved educational attainment. This required that children should arrive at school ready to learn, that is to say not hungry (Social Exclusion Unit 1998: 7) and that new ways be developed to motivate them to learn, to encourage them to appreciate that their own best interests would be served by regular school attendance and full participation in learning. The strategy 'Schools Plus' (Social Exclusion Unit 1998: 70) was appropriately named, since it involved an increase in the amount of time children would spend in the school environment. 'Homework centres' would occupy them after the normal school day, 'breakfast clubs' before the normal school day began, and 'summer schools' would occupy them during summer holidays (Social Exclusion Unit 1998: 71).

Bringing Britain Together was not intended as a stand-alone solution. It was one element of a broader set of strategies for tackling social problems. In 1998 the UK government passed the Crime and Disorder Act (Home Office 1998). This was a set of statutory provisions, changes to existing law and procedure, that formed a second wing of the government's overall strategy. The Act had particular significance for the 'out of place' children of deprived neighbourhoods. We shall now describe some of the provisions that the Crime and Disorder Act 1998 introduced, paying close attention to issues of being, becoming and ambiguity.

Sections 11–13 of the Act provide for Child Safety Orders (CSOs). The Act allows local authority social services departments to apply to a local magistrates' court for a CSO when a child under 10 has committed an act that would have led to their criminal prosecution if they were 10 or over, if a child under 10 had broken a 'local child curfew notice' (more on these later), or if such an order was thought necessary to prevent a child's 'antisocial behaviour'. If granted by the court, a CSO would lead to the appointment of a 'responsible officer' who would work to ensure that the child concerned receives appropriate care, protection and support and is subject to proper control. So, if a child slips out of the 'becoming' category, either by the failure of parents to live up to standard child-rearing expectations or by the child's rejection of adult authority, a CSO will provide a responsible officer whose task is effectively to redraw and reinstate the adult/child boundary. The CSO, then, is a strategy for converting an ambiguous child, whose activities contradict the standard image of a becoming, into a becoming for the purposes of reducing levels of antisocial behaviour, crime and fear of crime.

Sections 8–10 of the Act provide for Parenting Orders (POs). POs are designed 'to help and support parents or guardians in addressing their child's anti-social or offending behaviour' (Home Office 1998). If a PO is imposed by a court, the parent or guardian may be required to attend counselling or guidance sessions for up to three months, and will be encouraged to exercise a greater degree of control over the child's movements. This may involve ensuring that the child attends school or that the child avoids people or places that are taken to have contributed to their antisocial or offending behaviour. If parents under POs fail to meet these requirements they can be fined up to £1000. The PO, then, is a strategy for converting an ambiguous child, whose activities, movements and associations contradict the standard image of a becoming, into a becoming. It aims to achieve this by redrawing and reinstating the adult/child boundary, 'encouraging' parents to control their children. Once again the aim is to reduce antisocial behaviour, crime and fear of crime.

Sections 14–15 of the Act provide for local child curfews. Under the Act local governments can impose a curfew on children under 10 who are on the streets between 9 p.m. and 6 a.m. These curfews can last up to 60 days. If a child is found on the streets during the hours of curfew by a police officer they will be taken home. If there are no adults to take care of them at home, they will then be taken into police custody. A child breaking a curfew may also be placed under a CSO. Where CSOs and POs are applied to particular children, this provision reasserts the adult/child boundary across a whole neighbourhood. It effectively turns children's unsupervised presence on the streets into an instance of antisocial behaviour. The curfew deals with all children in a particular area in the same way, regardless of their actual conduct. Whether a given child is playing or vandalizing cars, a curfew treats them as equally suspicious. Under a curfew, it does not matter *which* children are removed from the streets as long as *some* children are removed from the streets. While this strategy does not treat children as subhuman, it is certainly a response to the image of the horde.

It is not surprising that a government should have such a concern for the preservation of social order. Since the fear of crime has been identified as a hindrance to the development of *good* social capital and community spirit, neither is it surprising that the Act introduces provisions to reclaim the streets for the community. It is striking, however, that current responses to urban deprivation focus so closely on children's conduct and movements. The policies that we have examined are intended to ensure that children stay in their proper place: school during the day and the family home at night. There is a recognition built into these policies that children are capable of independent action and movement. Throughout the legal provisions, and especially in the case of the local child curfew, there is a sense that such being-like behaviour is not to be allowed, and that children have to be made to live up to the role of becomings. The tension between ideals of childhood and realities has generated an ambiguity around the children of poor neighbourhoods in the UK, an ambiguity that is taken to threaten legitimate social order. For social order to be maintained, then, and for neighbourhoods to be renewed, children must become becomings.

Conclusion: children bearing the burden of uncertainty

In this chapter we have seen how the economic conditions of the late twentieth century and national and international policy responses to them have increased the incidence of children 'out of place'. The rise in numbers of such children is closely linked to the widening of the gap between rich and poor that has taken place in the age of uncertainty. While such children have been present on the city streets of the North (Cockburn 1995) and the South (Connolly and Ennew 1996) throughout the modern era, the recent rise in their numbers has made them newly visible. They have become the focus of policies and practices, both official and unofficial, aimed at strengthening social order in a period of rapid socio-economic change. These children constitute a problem for adult authorities like the police and local and national governments because while they cannot easily be seen as becomings, authorities that are invested in the ideals of the developmental state *cannot* recognize them as beings.

The ambiguity of poorer children has led, as we have seen, in some cases to their elimination and in others to the development of new policies aimed at enforcing their 'becoming' status more strictly. While there is no moral equivalence between Brazilian death squads of the early 1990s and late 1990s UK legislation, both are an attempt to preserve social order by controlling children. For all the differences in the economic position and social policies of the countries of the North and South, our examination of children 'out of place' brings us to one clear conclusion. In the age of uncertainty, the weight of adult problems of maintaining social order has come to rest on poor children. Their ambiguity puts them in the position to be blamed for social problems and to be treated as a well-spring of social disorder.

5

Children in their place: home, school and media

In the previous chapter, we charted the 'out of place' position of poorer children in the cities of the North and the South. We gave examples of how tensions between the ideal of childhood as protected dependency and real socio-economic conditions have made these children into ambiguous figures. Since they cannot easily be classified as human beings or as human becomings, children 'out of place' present a threat to social order in general, and to the order of the developmental state in particular. Rather than seeing the roots of this problem in poverty and social deprivation, and instead of questioning their ideals of childhood, adult authorities have tended to see the children themselves as the location of the problem, a subhuman horde or a cause of community decay. Since such children carry the burden of ambiguity, formal and informal practices have been developed either, as in early 1990s Brazil, to eliminate them, or, as in late 1990s UK, to reinforce their family life with renewed discipline and firmer boundaries so as to return them to a clear state of becoming.

Given the extremes of danger that a state of ambiguity can expose children to, and given the role of the 'becoming' ideal in generating this danger, small wonder that sociologists of childhood urge us, as we saw in Chapter 3, to redefine children as beings and to recognize them as such. Recognizing children as beings would, it seems, dispel the tension between developmental ideals and economic realities that creates ambiguity around poorer children in the first place. It would allow those children who are not strictly becomings nevertheless to have access to the cultural goods of dignity and respect due to those who have a clear identity. Given the strength and widespread acceptance of the model of the developmental state, we can see, however, that redefining children as beings is an enormous task. It has implications for family structure, for the pursuit of social order and for the very legitimacy of the relationship between states and their populations. Of course, just because a job is hard and complicated does not mean that it should be abandoned. But our argument so far suggests not only that the category 'human becoming' is problematic, but also that 'human being' is unclear, and, further, that the task of placing people into the categories 'being' and 'becoming', so central to the functioning of the developmental state, has become more difficult in the age of uncertainty. The masses of poor children, concentrated in towns and cities by modernization and then impoverished by a combination of economic recession and policy responses to it testify to the contemporary difficulties of maintaining a clear being/ becoming division. It would seem that global social change is rapidly making the traditional terms through which we understand 'growing up' difficult to maintain.

Now if childhood ambiguity was only to be found in the poorer parts of the world, we might be able to dismiss it simply as a result of accidental failures of the developmental state. We would be able to claim that for a large number of children (albeit still a global minority) the being/becoming division remains the best way to understand their lives. But what if forms of childhood ambiguity were also emerging in the well-ordered homes and schools of the wealthy? Perhaps then we could see childhood ambiguity as a positive tendency of the age of uncertainty rather than as a marginal phenomenon restricted to the economic fringes of the world. So, in this chapter we shall turn our attention to those children who are most clearly 'in their place', the wealthier children who spend their daytimes in school and their evenings at home. Although these children would seem to match the requirements of the developmental state perfectly, we shall see that there is ambiguity at work here too. We shall argue that late-twentieth-century social change, especially the proliferation of media technologies, such as television and new information and communication technologies (ICT), has created a being/becoming ambiguity *within* family homes and schools, the very bastions of the developmental state. While this sensitively located ambiguity has formed the basis of controversies over children's exposure to and use of media (Buckingham 2000), it is not always understood as problematic. Indeed, by the end of the chapter, it should be clear that childhood ambiguity in highly mediated societies can also be seen as *necessary* for the production of 'self-programming' (Castells 1996) adult citizens, who are capable of learning, changing and adapting throughout their lives: citizens fit, in other words, for the uncertainties of the new economy. In this sense, the ambiguity of childhood may even be seen as an operating principle of certain emergent technologically mediated educational practices. We shall begin to chart the childhood ambiguities of affluent societies, however, by examining the family home of the Fordist period, its role as the principal protected space for children, and its development as a site of consumption.

Ambiguity in the family home

The family home preferred within the developmental state can be described as a 'cocoon', a safe space in which the child is protected from the outside world. We saw examples of this cocooning in Chapter 2, when we asked how children came to be seen as dependent. This cocooning function of the family home, in development since the eighteenth century, was strengthened in a wave of social reconstruction that followed the Second World War. Across Europe, the war had brought mass displacements of children as evacuees and refugees, of men of fathering age as soldiers and the deployment of women as workers in war industries. Many elements of postwar reconstruction aimed at the restoration of a degree of family security and integration that had recently been disrupted. In the UK, for example, the passage of the Family Allowances Act in 1945 targeted welfare resources on families with children and, from 1945 onwards, a great deal of public-sector rented accommodation, carefully designed to house the two-generation family unit (parents and children), was built to replace bomb-damaged and slum housing (Pickvance 1999). The 'welfare states' that emerged across Europe during post-war reconstruction had the goal of repairing families, restoring safety for children and of making the protective cocoon stronger than ever before. The 'welfare state', then, had great implications for children's social position. Children were to be surrounded by many concentric layers of adult protection and guidance; first parents and their care, then the walls of the family home; then health and welfare workers and their expertise; then the state itself standing guard in case of parents' inability or failure to support their children.

The post-war period, as we saw in Chapter 1, also saw an economic boom across western industrial nations. Relatively low levels of unemployment and a relatively high degree of job security helped to reproduce a 'traditional' division of labour between adult men and women, a division of labour that had been put in question by many women's wartime occupation in industry. The work of industrial production was placed in men's hands, while reproductive labour (child-rearing) and the labour of consumption (shopping, cooking and cleaning) were assigned to women. As this division of adult labour became clearer, the cocoon around children took on two parallel, gendered forms. Fathers earned wages outside the family, mediating between children and the adult world of work and production, while mothers mediated between children and the adult world of consumption, keeping the household supplied with life's essentials. Childhood, then, in the immediate post-war years, was being shaped as a period of total protection and innocence. The family home was being shaped as a private space in which children's contact with the public world of work and commerce was filtered and mediated by adults. The post-war years, however, were not without their discontents.

The trivialization of the domestic

Throughout the Fordist period, from 1945 to the early 1970s, the gendered divisions of labour coupled with the privacy of the family home generated a new range of problems for women. Accounts of these problems arose first in the USA. Friedan (1963) noted how the family home, with its protective privacy, had given rise to a complex of secrecy. She described the lifestyle of many relatively affluent married women as involving a 'feminine mystique'. This mystique was intimately connected with women's almost exclusive responsibility for household consumption and child-rearing. For a woman properly to mediate consumption for her husband and children, all signs of her labour, of cleaning, food preparation and the sheer effort involved in child-rearing had to be concealed, otherwise the 'bad news' of the world of consumption and reproductive labour would penetrate the cocoon and the home would lose its innocence. For Friedan (1963), as for later feminist commentators (for example Greer 1971), this secrecy of household practice was accompanied by an interior psychological practice of concealment – the repression of female sexuality. In the post-war home, women, in so far as they lived the 'feminine mystique', were required to 'infantilize' themselves, to engage in a work of concealment, hiding such traces of their adulthood as evidence of their labour and evidence of their sexual desire. The more concealed the labour of consumption, childcare and sexuality could be, the more innocent and protective the space of the family home could appear. An ideal home was one in which, to all appearances, nothing of great significance happened. Thus, along with the concealment of labour within the family home, along with the innocence of the home, came the trivialization of matters of consumption, of women and of children.

It is important to note here that this trivialization of women and children depended on the viability of Fordist production, since it depended on men's ability to lay almost exclusive claim to the status of breadwinner. As long as Fordist socio-economic arrangements held, it seems, the family home could remain a space of 'innocence', and all within it could remain trivial, seen as dependent, infantile and innocent. But as Harvey (1989) argues, Fordist socio-economic arrangements were not only about production. As we saw in Chapter 1, for Fordism to remain stable, mass markets had to be found for the goods it mass produced. So Fordism was also about mass consumption.

Consumer society

In the relatively prosperous 1950s and 1960s many ordinary families in the industrial west could afford to purchase or to rent consumer goods such as washing machines, refrigerators, vacuum cleaners and television sets. Some of these devices were designed to cut down on domestic labour, to allow for higher standards of household order for a smaller expenditure of effort.

Washing machine, refrigerator and vacuum cleaner reinforced the mystique of the household. Each in their own way made it easier to conceal the traces of the domestic labour of consumption. Steamy sinks of suds were replaced with a humming white box. Another white box decreased both the speed and the visibility of milk turning sour. The vacuum cleaner collected dust from carpets and other fabrics without sending a cloud of residual dust into the air.

But these devices had an impact beyond concealment. They also increased the diversity of goods (food stuffs and clothing) that could be stored, preserved and maintained within the family home. Washing machine, refrigerator and vacuum cleaner were vital pieces of equipment for expanding the range of purchasing choices. In the well-equipped home, the labour of consumption expanded from the gathering and maintenance of necessities to the formulation of decisions over what to purchase. In the consumer society, because the family home was increasingly open to the storage and maintenance of a wide range of goods, it came to function as a key, active relay in the economy. It was no longer just a site of consumption but became the principal locus of consumer *choice*. Since Fordist stability depended on mass consumption as well as mass production, consumption within the family home became a matter of *serious* interest. The family home began to take on a significance of its own as a site of consumption and choice. One domestic appliance in particular, the television, would secure the economic significance of the family home, and, as it did so, would also subtly alter children's status.

Television was the ideal form of entertainment for a cocooning family. It could be enjoyed without leaving the home and in tandem with families' enjoyment of other home comforts made available by domestic appliances. But, whether through the set design of fictional programming, or through advertisements, the television acted as a 'shop window', presenting the bounty and diversity of the consumer society to consumers in their own homes. Television was a technology that brought news of the outside world into the home, the news that the family home and its gendered division of labour had, till now, filtered out in order to preserve children's 'innocence'. While being a key element of the cocoon, television brought about a penetration of that cocoon. Television interfered with the household structure of secrecy and with the trivialization of the domestic sphere. This was to have significant implications for the nature of childhood and for children's social position. As we shall see, the conditions of consumer society provided new opportunities for children to demonstrate independence of mind relative to their carers.

The disappearance of childhood?

One commentator summarized the effects of television on childhood as follows: 'Without secrets, of course, there can be no such thing as childhood' (Postman 1983: 80). Postman argues that television shattered the secrecy and privacy of the home, thereby destroying 'childhood'. Television, the 'total disclosure medium' (Postman 1983: 81), makes all images of the adult world equally available to children and adults. For Postman, television competes with adults in their role as media or mediators for their children. It thus threatens the innocence of childhood. But Postman (1983) argues further that without this difference in the availability of information, without the filtering of information by adults, there can be no real difference between adult and child. The structure of secrecy that separated and protected children from the adult world, the very essence of childhood, was wiped out by television. The implication is that there are no more becomings. Though Postman's claim that television has made childhood 'disappear' is rather extreme, and though we might not want to share his 'anti-television' stance, it is, as we shall see, quite clear that television has changed children's position within the family home, gradually reducing their 'triviality' as consumer society developed.

We have argued that in the consumer society, the family home had become a key economic relay. Television exposed children in the family home to the availability of goods and to the possibility of making choices between goods. Children have always played an economic role as *recipients* of the benefits of adult labour and have received the effects of activities undertaken on their behalf by caregivers. Those making purchasing decisions always had to bear children in mind. But children's exposure to choice and diversity through the medium of television means that, within consumer society, children's *minds* have to be borne in mind when purchasing decisions are made. Exposure to choice gives children a position from which to have a say in purchasing decisions. It thus allows them to have a significant impact on the economy. In this context, children are no longer trivial, no longer simply becomings to be protected, but also beings to be respected. Buckingham (2000) provides us with plenty of evidence that, by the late twentieth century, the children of affluent societies had become major economic players. For example, children can influence adults' purchasing decisions through 'pester power' (Buckingham 2000: 147); it has been estimated that $130 billion of household purchases in the USA are significantly influenced by children's preferences every year (Buckingham 2000: 147). Children also form a market in their own right. In the USA this market is worth around $10 billion each year (Buckingham 2000: 147). We might imagine that children's purchasing choices were restricted to toys and games, and indeed these sectors have grown rapidly throughout the late twentieth century, but children also have influence over the increasingly important market for information and communication technologies (ICTs), such as personal computers and mobile phones. As Buckingham (2000) writes:

> In the UK, the take-up of satellite and cable television, video, camcorders and home computers is proportionally much higher in households with children: 35 per cent of households with children

now subscribe to cable or satellite television, for example, as compared with 25 per cent overall; while 90 per cent of households with
children have access to a VCR (video cassette recorder) as compared
with 75 per cent overall.

(Buckingham 2000: 83)

Disappearance or complexity?

So how are we to understand children's economic role as consumers in
terms of human being and human becoming? Have affluent children left
the state of 'becoming' behind, as Postman suggests? For Postman (1983),
childhood has disappeared, the loss of secrecy has emptied the 'becoming'
category and only human beings are left. But Buckingham's (2000) view is
more subtle and complex. We can expect no clear answer to the question of
whether children are now beings or becomings, because within the family
home of the consumer society, children are *both* beings and becomings.
Childhood has not 'disappeared', it has rather become more complex and
ambiguous. Children are still cocooned within the family home, but that
home also opens on to a world of consumer choice in which they are
important players in their own right. In this sense, the children of the
affluent west, thanks largely to the development of the present day's highly
mediated consumer society, are now both dependent and independent. They
effectively have dual status as becomings and as beings.

If the post-war social and economic settlement began by increasing the
cocooning of affluent children, increasing the degree to which they fit
the standards of the developmental state, it also contained the seeds for the
development of childhood ambiguity within the family home. Mass production required mass consumption. Mass consumption involved greater
consumer choice, and, largely through the medium of television, children
gained access to information that enabled them to make consumer choices.
This gave them access to a degree of independent choice-making and influence that now coexists alongside their dependency. Even though they
remain 'in their place', wealthier children are now significant participants
in the economy, playing a part in driving the markets for ICTs that are so
central to the new economy.

Childhood ambiguity, then, is not restricted to the poorer parts of the
world. Forms of childhood ambiguity, admittedly different in kind, have
emerged from wealth and poverty alike. It seems that childhood ambiguity
cannot be dismissed as a marginal phenomenon or as an accidental failure.
Whether it is to be found in the lives of the rich or the poor, and whether
we think its effects are deplorable or desirable, this ambiguity is a vital
feature of contemporary childhoods. The more significant this ambiguity
becomes, the less value the traditional terms of being and becoming are
likely to have in understanding children's social positions and the nature of
'growing up'.

Having discussed the emergence and significance of childhood ambiguity in the home, we can now turn to the other 'proper' place for children within the developmental state – the school – and ask whether contemporary schoolchildren in the affluent west can be described as 'beings' or 'becomings'.

Ambiguity at school

As we saw in Chapter 2, education was a key element of the modern developmental state. It was and, for the most part, remains an area of social life in which children are understood and treated as sites of investment, as human becomings requiring special treatment. So we owe the 'becoming' view of children largely to the historical processes of state development in western Europe. Yet the details, purposes and outcomes of educational practice have changed over the centuries. Once, the teacher cut an all-knowing, all-powerful figure within the classroom. Teachers' authority was based on their status as completed beings, full of certain knowledge. Teachers' authority was starkly opposed to children's lack of autonomy within the classroom – a feature of their status as incomplete becomings. The stark contrast between adult being and child becoming is now no longer such a key feature of schools in the affluent west. As the question of what knowledge a child should be given has become harder to answer – as journey's end (see Chapter 1) has receded from view – the practical details and purposes of education have changed. The figure of the pupil is changing from a passive, docile *recipient* of adult knowledge and expertise to an active and relatively independent *creator* of information.

As we shall see, however, ours is not a simple story of the gradual recognition of children's status as human beings within education. Rather it tells how the social practices of schooling first created and enforced a passive, docile becoming role for pupils and then, in the mid-twentieth century, came to incorporate a recognition of children's activity as learners, treating them as 'active' becomings. Whether passive or active learners, however, children in these arrangements were still seen as being on their way to completion, to a finished state of adulthood. But as we turn to the present day, we shall see that while the being/becoming division was once clear enough to act as the theoretical and practical basis of schooling, the use of information and communication technology in education is now opening teacher and pupil alike to a new flexibility.

Instead of a gradual incorporation of children into the 'being' category, then, our account of educational change will point out the decreasing relevance of the oppositional terms 'being' and 'becoming'. By the end of our account it should be clear that, as ICT is incorporated into education, schoolchildren in the affluent west fit less easily into either the 'being' or 'becoming' categories. This is another example of what we have so far called 'childhood ambiguity'. But our examination of education will allow us to say something more. Children in schools are still sites of investment, they are still involved in processes of becoming, but this becoming increasingly resembles a 'becoming without end', a form of changing and learning that has no final destination. We shall also suggest that teachers and the adult population in general are coming to share this state of 'becoming without end'. We begin our account in the origins of the modern school as a social organization and with the creation of the 'passive becoming' as the model of the pupil.

Docile pupils and passive becoming

For the historian and philosopher Michel Foucault (1977), the school is one among a number of 'disciplinary' institutions that developed in modernity. On his account, the school, like the prison, the factory and the army barracks, developed from the seventeenth and eighteenth centuries as institutions for shaping people's conduct to clear purposes. The school was a place in which skills and information were conveyed from teacher to pupil. But it was also a sophisticated technology which produced day-to-day order within its own walls, made comparisons between pupils' individual performance and general standards of competence, and charted pupils' progress against time. In other words, as we shall see, the disciplinary school was a machine for making 'passive becomings'.

The most basic objective of disciplinary schooling was to ensure that pupils in a class were quiet, settled and ready to learn. In other words, techniques had to be devised and implemented to ensure that the pupils were 'docile' (Foucault 1977: 136). Misbehaviour, ranging from distracting other pupils, through talking out of turn, to simple inattention, had to be prevented for the school's clear educational purpose to be met. So, all forms of conduct that pupils could undertake in independence of the teacher's intentions and commands were problematic. Clearly, pupils had different characters and abilities, had friendships with, and likes and dislikes among their peers. They had lives of their own. They could thus become bored with or interested in their lessons at different times from each other, and were capable of distracting each other's attention from the lesson at hand. The early modern teacher faced a basic problem of order. How were all the diverse characters, interests and relationships of the pupils to be managed in order that they could be taken steadily through their lesson? How could a diverse and active group of people be turned into a quiescent 'class'? One possibility was for the teacher to threaten physical punishment for misbehaviour. This was certainly a feature of early modern schooling. But Foucault (1977) draws our attention to less dramatic techniques for making an active mass of children with their own purposes and interests into a docile class bent on the single purpose of education.

The techniques deployed in the creation of passive becomings were rather mundane, but proved so effective that you might recognize them from your own school days. Classrooms were designed so that each child had a specific place to sit, their own chair, or place on a bench, and their own area of desk space. These individual spaces were arranged to face the front of the classroom. This simple spacing of children as individuals, fixed in place in lines facing the teacher, allowed the teacher easily to see when a child was moving out of their place, leaning toward their neighbour, say, or passing a note. A grid of proper places was thereby established giving the teacher the means to make quick decisions about whether or not some misbehaviour was occurring or was about to occur. With all the pupils aligned in the same posture, it was even easier to tell from small deviations in posture – slumping or leaning – whether a given child was attending to the lesson or not. The earlier a teacher could intervene with a word of caution or a fresh command, the less often serious misbehaviour would develop, and the less often lessons would have to be interrupted for a child to be punished. So a crucial part of running an efficient classroom was the systematic exclusion of the possibility of children's independent activity. A mass of people with their own interests, desires and personal likes and dislikes was thereby disciplined into an orderly collection of pupils who, for the most part, would then abandon their own activities to be led, passively, by the teacher.

So the problem of classroom order was tackled by the imposition of a spatial grid, which, coupled with the teacher's checks and admonishments, turned each pupil from an element of a disorderly mass, into a discrete docile individual. Simple ordering techniques were also developed to regulate pupils' learning over time. Curricula were devised that broke the skills or information to be learned into small chunks. Foucault illustrates this with an eighteenth-century scheme that broke the process of learning to read into seven distinct levels:

> the first for those who are beginning to learn the letters, the second for those who are learning to spell, the third for those who are learning to join syllables together to form words.
>
> (Foucault 1977: 159)

. . . and so on. With a skill, task or set of information broken into levels of increasing difficulty, it was then possible for the teacher to test all pupils at the end of each level. Such examinations could thus be used to determine the rank of each pupil in the class (giving a comparative measure of each child's competence) and to determine the rate of progress of each child through the curriculum. This information made it possible to establish standard expectations for children's achievement over time and to chart individual children's deviation from standard. So not only did disciplinary schooling produce passive, docile students, but also it provided information on the speed and success of their 'becoming' competent. At the centre of these orderings of space and time, stood the teacher, coordinating pupil, task and curriculum, to turn an undiscriminated mass of people with their own lives, desires and interests into an homogeneous class of passive becomings. The teacher had power and authority over the pupils as long as pupils' conduct was regulated and aligned with the teacher's purposes. Thus the creation of passive becomings for the single purpose of education was also the creation of a form of adult expertise over children as becomings. Education was closely linked with adult authority and children's obedience.

Child-centred schooling and active becomings

While many of the educational practices Foucault describes are still with us, and children are still widely tested and ranked according to ability, the early modern emphasis on the passivity of the pupil was to be challenged in the mid-twentieth century. Disciplinary education, with its key features of passive pupils and high levels of spatial and temporal ordering, was exported from the west to the 'developing world' just as were industrialization and the model of the developmental state. By the late 1960s, however, Illich (1971) and Lister (1974) were questioning the suitability of disciplinary schooling for 'developing' nations. Disciplinary schooling called for resources, such as teachers and schoolrooms, that were expensive and therefore in short supply. It was geared to producing adults who were accomplished at passing examinations, but who did not necessarily have many practical skills. The argument was that passive becomings were a luxury that 'developing' nations could not afford and, perhaps, did not need. The argument for 'deschooling' society, for breaking the connection between education and rigid adult authority, was also extended to the west, as part of a broad cultural movement for the liberation of individual potential. As long as education was associated with adult authority, the majority of schoolchildren, it seemed, were being trained simply to take orders. So the connections between teachers' authority and pupils' passivity that had seemed so necessary for orderly and efficient education were now under question. In the midst of this mid-century debate, new child-centred forms of education were being developed and tested. They drew inspiration from, among other sources, Piaget's theories of child development (Walkerdine 1984).

In Chapter 3, we examined Piaget's (1955) psychological theories of child development quite closely in order to illustrate the 'dominant framework' that has recently drawn so much criticism from sociologists of childhood. One of the crucial elements of Piaget's (1955) theory was that, in order to develop, children had to have plenty of information about the world around them and opportunities to 'work' on that information. The developing child is far from passive in Piaget's (1955) scheme. Since the information children receive about the world is often contradictory and confusing, in order to gain a true appreciation of the nature of the world and of their place in it, children have to *work* on the raw information they receive through their senses, forming hypotheses about the world and gradually coming to a realistic, rational and adult understanding. For Piaget (1955), children are key players in their own development. If they are to develop into rational beings, they need the freedom to gather information, to draw their own conclusions and to think for themselves.

As we have seen, disciplinary schooling was based on rendering children as passive as possible, on cutting down their movements and interactions within the classroom grid. It was based on an attempt to limit the range of children's classroom experiences to hearing the words and watching the actions of the teacher. While it offered teachers the convenience of a docile class, this approach came to look quite mistaken in the light of Piaget's (1955) work. Further, structured curricula and day-to-day educational practice had long taken note of the different levels of difficulty inherent in the knowledge and skills children were to learn. The introduction of Piaget's (1955) insights into educational practice was to add an awareness of the different levels of capability inherent in children as they aged. Children's minds now had to be borne in mind. So, rather than leading passive pupils through the curriculum, the 'child-centred' teacher would have the dual task of presenting children with age-appropriate experiences and helping them actively to think about those experiences.

The pupil of child-centred education was still a 'becoming'. Indeed their status as becomings was now recognized as psychological fact. But they were conceived of as *active* rather than passive becomings. The relative merits of teacher-focused and child-focused educational practices, seen in the light of Piaget's work, was neatly summarized as follows: 'I hear and I forget. I see and I remember. I do and I understand' (Nuffield Foundation cited in Walkerdine 1984: 155).

This invocation of the power of active involvement in learning comes from the highly influential book *I Do and I Understand* (Nuffield Foundation 1967), which shaped infant and primary school education (5–11-year-olds) in the UK throughout the 1970s, and had effects that have lasted to the present day. Walkerdine's (1984) study of the child-centred approach reveals that the conception of the child as an active becoming, who needed opportunities to 'do' in order to 'understand', was accompanied by changes in standard classroom layout, changes designed to give children many opportunities to become active learners. The grid-like space of the old-fashioned classroom was broken up into a number of different areas, each of which could make a contribution to activating children as learners. Rows of desks facing the teacher were replaced with separate tables where a few children might sit facing each other. This allowed children to interact with one another. Rather than being seen as a threat to the teacher's control, this arrangement was recommended as providing opportunities for children to develop social skills and competences. Cupboards containing equipment for children's hands-on learning activities – mathematical toys and art and craft materials – were used like walls to mark off special spaces for reading, woodwork and model-making. This new design was so committed to children's activity, freedom of movement and of experience within the classroom that it even included a space reserved for 'sudden and unpredictable' interests and activities (Walkerdine 1984: 157).

The child-centred approach to education was intended to give children a context in which to have rich and diverse social, material and informational experiences to interest, engage and puzzle them, and thereby to nourish their active self-development. As we have already noted, it not only produced the novel role of active becomings, but also altered the relationship between education and adult authority. Where the teacher had been the literal and metaphorical focus of the traditional classroom, at once the centre of control and of knowledge, child-centred education broke the link between adult authority and educational practice. The child-centred teacher was a guide for children and a facilitator of their experience and reflection rather than a leader equipped with all necessary knowledge. To be a teacher, it was no longer necessary to be 'complete', nor was it desirable to have complete control of children's attention or activities.

As influential as the child-centred approach was, it certainly did not amount to a total revolution in schooling experience across the globe, across the affluent west or even in the UK. Its application beyond the education of 5–11-year-olds, for example, has been limited by its tendency to reduce teachers' classroom control function. It threatens traditional conceptions of good behaviour and discipline. Debates still continue over the issue of how active and free children should be allowed to be in schools. These are often conducted in terms of preferences for 'traditional' methods as against 'progressive' methods, pitting common sense against developmental expertises (Elvin 1977). The question of whether teachers *should* be authority figures, of whether education needs to be based on the dominance of an adult over a group of children is very much alive. But as we shall now see, the central features of the child-centred approach – stimulating children's active learning and decoupling adult authority from the business of education – are being taken up and repeated in a rather different context, that of the use of ICT in education.

Becomings without end?

The term 'information and communication technology' covers all the new media that have been made possible through the increasing power and decreasing costs of computing in the late twentieth century. At the time of writing, the dominant form of ICT is the networked personal computer (PC). Hooked up to a telephone line, the PC becomes an interface between the user and 'servers' around the world, devices that store and send information. Together, networked PCs, servers and telephone lines allow users to search for and to access information from around the world, without leaving their desks. Along with the transmission of pictures and text, goods and services can also be ordered and paid for through such media. As Castells (1996) argues, this increasingly easy and rapid transmission of information is a driving force behind the development of the new economy. It increases the reach of commercial organizations, widens the spread of their potential market, and thus increases the intensity and speed of competition between them. ICT, then, is a crucial element of the flexibilization of the economy and of people's lives. It helps to shorten the length of time between a knowable present and an unpredictable future. It is thus a key feature of our age of uncertainty.

One thing that does seem clear, however, is that if the amount of business conducted through ICT is going to increase, then those countries whose populations have access to it and are familiar with using it are more likely to flourish in the new economy. Just as industrial societies needed numerate and literate populations, so information societies will need ICT-competent populations. This need has been a significant influence on educational policy in the UK during the 1980s and 1990s (Somekh 2000). A host of initiatives are currently focused on developing a National Grid for Learning, installing PCs and telecommunications lines to ensure that pupils are able to access the world wide web as part of their everyday school experience. By 2002, more than £700 million will have been spent on hardware, software, internet connections and services for UK schools (Somekh 2000).

The reasoning behind this pattern of investment in schools will be familiar. Investments in ICT are being made in the expectation of future national advantage. The intention is to ensure that the future population is equipped to compete economically, to help 'with the vital task of keeping Britain competitive in the 21st century' (Michael Heseltine quoted in Somekh 2000). Children, it seems, 'cannot be effective in tomorrow's world if they are trained in yesterday's skills' (Tony Blair quoted in Somekh 2000).

But what do children need to learn through ICT? What skills will they be developing to equip them for future economic competition? There are the basics, such as familiarity with operating networked PCs, and the ability to recognize the range of different forms of communication they allow, such as email, online discussion groups and websites. Familiarity with these new forms of communication can be developed by shifting basic writing and reading tasks from paper textbooks and exercise books to the screen. ICT resources, however, are quite unlike textbooks. Textbooks are highly structured media. They carry an authorized version of what children need to know. The information they carry has been pre-selected for the child to fit clear educational purposes. But the global network of information is relatively unstructured. If you issue a request for information on 'child development', for example, you are likely to receive a list of thousands of web-pages from universities, commercial organizations, charities and individuals, made available for a wide range of campaigning, promotional and educational purposes. To find specific facts or theories takes a much more selective search. Because ICT gives easy access to a large amount of relatively unstructured information, ICT competence consists of the ability to locate the information that one actually requires by imposing one's own filters and structures on what has been made available. ICT then presents a medium that demands that the user be active in making choices and decisions. Consequently, ICT education is not so much about children internalizing sets of pre-selected facts and figures, deemed important by authoritative adults, but, rather, focuses on developing children's ability to 'wrap' the world of information around themselves, to filter and manage it for their own purposes.

For Somekh (2000) one of the most significant consequences of the introduction of ICT to schools is a change in the relationship between teacher and pupil. If pupils are to learn how to control information flow, to 'wrap' information around themselves, then teachers must first relinquish part of their control over them. This means that the teacher

> is no longer sharply separated from the student by role, with one imparting knowledge and the other imbibing it. Instead: There is . . . an understanding that teaching and learning are independent aspects of a single activity . . . Teachers cast themselves in the role of a learner or co-learner *at the same time* as that of a teacher (emphasis in orginal).
>
> (Somekh 2000: 28)

So ICT, together with governmental and educators' responses to it, has the ability to decouple adult authority from the business of education, increasingly casting the pupil as an active participant in their own learning. In place of a clear discrimination between adult being and child becoming, then, we are seeing an increasing ambiguity in childhood within the networked school. But there is a further significant change in progress. Children are not being taught ICT competences so that they can *stop* learning when they have finished the curriculum. There is no state of 'completion' or 'journey's end' in view. Rather children are being taught so that they can *continue* to learn and to change after school, so that they are ready to adapt to future unpredictable demands and circumstances. For Somekh (2000) the habits of staying in touch with a changing world, of wrapping that world around one's plans and interests, and of continuing to do so as one plans and interests change, will be vital to future economic success. Where industrial societies of the past needed completed beings who could competently fill stable and predictable roles, information societies need 'self-confident, independent thinkers . . . capable of acquiring a range of different skills and adapting to several jobs over a lifetime' (Somekh 2000: 35).

The introduction of ICT in schools is instrumental in changing the purposes of education. There is a trend away from the conversion of incomplete becomings into completed beings and toward the activation of 'becomings without end'.

We have seen how the introduction of ICT to education has the potential to change the nature of pupil–teacher relationships within schools and thereby to increase childhood's ambiguity. We have also seen how closely these changes are related to governmental and educational understandings of the demands of the age of uncertainty. But the effects of these changes are not limited to children in schools. Responses to the new economy at the level of the European Commission have begun to identify a state of 'becoming without end' as a new standard for European citizens. Adults must remain open and unfinished even as they become economically active. They must retain 'the capacity to learn how to learn' (Edwards 1997: 32). The key document here is the European Commission publication entitled *Teaching and Learning: Towards a Learning Society* (Commission of the European Communities 1995). This policy discussion document identifies a need for 'continuous adjustment to skills and attitudes in a rapidly changing society' (Commission of the European Communities 1995: 20). Edwards (1997) makes it clear just how much current debate and actual and projected change in the provision of adult training and education is geared toward maintaining and supporting the readiness and ability of adults to remain flexible and adaptable.

Conclusion

In this chapter we have seen how family homes and schools were once built around a clear distinction between adult being and child becoming. We saw that this distinction depended to a large extent on adults' ability to mediate and to control children's experiences and access to information. The family home could be seen as an innocent and protective space for children as long as adults stood between children and the wider world, mediating and filtering on their behalf. Further, schooling, both in its disciplinary and child-centred forms has operated as a 'machine' for converting children into becomings, whether active or passive. Once again, adult control over children's experience and access to information were central to maintenance of the being/becoming distinction. But new forms of technological mediation, coupled with new practices of consumption and education have altered the possibility and desirability of maintaining a clear identity for children as becomings. So we have argued that changes in the central institutions of the developmental state, the family home and the school, are making the principle distinction of the developmental state, that between beings and becomings, less and less pertinent to the understanding of children's lives. In both home and school, children in the affluent west are coming to occupy a dual status as both becomings and beings. So from the perspective of anyone using the being/becoming division to understand 'growing up', childhood is becoming increasingly ambiguous.

We have already raised the question of how we are to study childhood when the states of being and becoming and the opposition between them are fading from relevance. The accounts offered in this chapter have increased the pertinence of this question. But beyond the increasing ambiguity of childhood, we have also seen the emergence of 'becoming without end', in both the figure of the pupil in the networked school and the adult in the learning society. Far from emptying the category 'human becoming' and making it possible to recognize everyone, regardless of age, as a human being, recent social change is leading to an abandonment of the category 'human being', an abandonment of the notions of completeness, stability and journey's end. The condition of human becoming is spreading throughout the life-course. But as it spreads, its meaning changes subtly. It no longer has a fixed location in the earlier years of life. It is quite unlike a traditional state of human becoming, because it has no end and can potentially be distributed throughout the life-course.

It is hoped that the nature and significance of this change is now clear. But the issues of how to think about children and childhood within these new conditions and of what research questions we can now pose about children and childhoods still need to be addressed. So in Chapter 7 we shall turn to the task of rethinking 'becoming' for the age of uncertainty in order to discover concepts that can help us to study children and childhoods in such a potentially confusing context. In Chapter 6, however, we shall examine the significance of childhood ambiguity in yet another context. We shall see that children's historical status as 'becomings' is still affecting their ability to speak and to be heard in formal, institutional decision-making processes. But we shall also see how new patterns of the mediation of children's voices are emerging, making new possibilities for children to be heard as speaking for themselves.

6

New places for children: voice, rights and decision-making

In the previous chapter, we saw how new media technologies have played a part in blurring distinctions between human being and human becoming. Television gave children the opportunity to play an active role in the economy from within the family home, making them at once 'dependent' and 'independent'. In UK schools, computer-based ICT is decreasing the emphasis on teacher's control over children's access to information. Both media are turning places of 'becoming' into places of ambiguity. We also saw that control over the information and experiences available to children have long been a central feature of their human becoming. Disciplinary schooling, for example, was able to turn children into docile becomings because its classroom grid increased teacher's ability to control their movements and experiences within the classroom, so as to direct their attention to the lesson at hand. Further, the privacy of the family home and, thus, the cocooned innocence of childhood, depended on adult caregivers' ability to filter information coming from the outside world. So the day-to-day details of the 'preservation' of children have, to a large extent, been about controlling children's access to information. This concern with information control reaches back through history to eighteenth-century warnings about the dangers of ghost stories told by nurses to children (see Chapter 2) and forward to contemporary concerns about the suitability of television and internet content for children (see Chapter 5).

It is not our purpose here to argue that such control is misguided, or that the preservation of children within the state of human becoming has done children more harm than good over the centuries. The accounts given in previous chapters should indicate that such sweeping judgements are ill advised. However, one side-effect of the informational preservation of children does require critical attention. The informational control of becoming has helped to *silence* children relative to adults. As the 'dependent becomings' of the developmental state (see Chapter 2) and as the 'incomplete becomings' of the dominant framework (see Chapter 3), children have, over the years, been deprived of voices of their own.

In this chapter we shall examine these issues of voice and silence. First, we shall give a brief account of how the silencing of children has occurred – how it makes sense within, and arises from, the terms of the developmental state and the dominant framework. We shall then see that the silencing of children is now widely recognized, in principle, as unjust. It makes it difficult for children to defend themselves from, or seek protection from, abuse and exploitation, and sets unnecessary limits on their participation in making decisions that affect their lives. We shall then discuss two examples of attempts to give children voice, to create places in which and from which children can speak for themselves. Our first example is Article 12 of the UN Convention on the Rights of the Child (General Assembly of the UN 1989); our second is the changing position of child witnesses in the criminal courts of England and Wales.

As we describe these attempts to give children voice, it should become clear that just as children 'out of place' and children 'in their place' are surrounded by ambiguity over their status, so a being/becoming ambiguity also attends these attempts to *change* children's place. In both cases we shall see that forms of childhood ambiguity complicate attempts to 'recognize' children as speakers in their own right. But we shall also be developing a theme from Chapter 4 – the notion of the *distribution* of the burden of ambiguity. Just as children 'out of place' came to bear the burden of childhood ambiguity, and were treated as the focus and origin of society's problems, so we shall see that the burden of ambiguity can also come to rest on children as they give voice. We shall argue that it is possible to *redistribute* the burden of childhood ambiguity, to take it off children's shoulders and share it more widely. As we conclude, we shall suggest that if the age of uncertainty is generating childhood ambiguity, then the study of how the burden of that ambiguity is distributed and redistributed is becoming a crucial concern for the social study of children and childhood. The study of childhood ambiguity, as we have seen, addresses questions of who carries the blame for social problems. As we shall see in this chapter, it can also address issues of the distribution of human dignity and recognition. But first, how has the silencing of children taken place? How is it that rights to speak and to be heard came to belong to adults, but not to children?

Who knows best?

We have seen that techniques for the control, filtering and mediation of information have been central to the preservation of children. We have also argued that the roots of the category 'human becoming' lie in those techniques. This has consequences beyond the informational and experiential 'inputs' that children receive. It also governs the reception of their 'outputs'. As long as children's experience and knowledge is controlled to a large degree by adults, be they teachers or caregivers, then adults can think of themselves as 'knowing more' than children. For Postman (1983), remember, this inequality of information – the existence of secrets – is the very essence of childhood. To his mind, the defence of childhood as a discrete period of the life-course depends on the preservation of adult's superiority as 'knowers'.

Now, if all the information that reaches a child has first passed through an adult, as it would if the informational preservation of children had been perfected, then everything the child knows is known second-hand. As long as children are dependent, protected and cocooned, everything the child can say can be said better, more completely, by an adult. Following this reasoning, there would simply never be cause to consult a child about any important matter. The child's voice could safely be ignored, because it could always be replaced by more reliable, adult sources. So, the control of children's access to information and experience over the years has made it easy for adults to ignore them. If what a child is saying happens to be important, it would seem that an adult probably knows it already, so the more dependent children are the less their 'voices' are likely to be heard and listened to.

We can see signs of this 'silencing' of children throughout the history of the developmental state. Though children formed the majority of the population in the disciplinary classroom, they were not consulted about the content or shape of the curriculum. Indeed, the classroom was designed to ensure children's silence, along with their passivity. When Chamoussett (see Chapter 2) planned to turn orphans into soldiers, he was not interested in what those orphans might have wanted for themselves, but was concerned merely to give them a place in reasons of state. At the high-water mark of the developmental state, after the Second World War, children, their views, opinions and knowledge, were as trivialized as those of anyone else who 'belonged' in the family home. So the developmental state has allowed and even encouraged adults to ignore or to discount what children say.

Are children capable of 'speaking for themselves'?

It is clear that the developmental state gave adults licence to ignore children. But there is a further, more *active* element to this silencing. The dominant framework gives us reasons to doubt whether children are even *capable* of speaking for themselves. Within the terms of the dominant framework, children, unlike adults, speak from, and for, ignorance and unreason. For Parsons (1956), children were simply ignorant of the vital conventions of their societies. Before they can participate fully in social life, before they can say anything worth hearing, they need to be socialized. When a child speaks, they necessarily speak out of ignorance of social convention. Turning to Piaget (1955), though his theories of cognitive development were based on his many conversations with children, what he heard from them convinced him only of children's fundamental difference from adults, their distance from reason. Having incomplete minds, children were unlikely to give voice to anything except further evidence of their incompleteness. Within the dominant framework, then, only human beings have voices that are properly their own. Since children are becomings, they cannot properly be said to speak for themselves, rather they speak from and for ignorance and unreason. Only the fully socialized or rational adults who have received the supplements necessary to lift them from nature's inadequacy, are capable of speaking *for themselves*.

Why should this concern us?

Why would it matter if children are not recognized as having voices of their own? If adults could be relied upon already to know whatever children know, and if they were as complete in their understanding of social convention and in their rationality as the dominant framework would suggest, then children's silencing would probably not be a problem at all. Under those conditions, adults would always know what children needed, perhaps before children themselves knew; they would have a complete understanding of the rights and wrongs of how to treat children, derived from their awareness of social convention; and they would have the rational faculties to decide how best to achieve those ends on children's behalf. These assumptions about adults' knowledge, abilities and moral competence are the very basis of the perceived legitimacy of adults' control over children's lives. If we can assume that these assumptions hold good, then we can assume that it is right for adults always to mediate on behalf of children and right for children always to be seen and not heard.

Unfortunately, the failings of adults and adult institutions to live up to these principles are, today, all too apparent. Adults cannot always be relied upon to understand children's needs or to pursue their best interests. Sometimes individual adults physically or sexually abuse children. Sometimes states leave children in poverty or expose them to the dangers of war, sickness and hunger. We might think of such abuses as accidental exceptions to the protective and preserving role of adults within the developmental state. But, as we saw in Chapter 2, the developmental state was not born out of a pure concern for children's well-being. The early pattern of investment in children was primarily a matter of the efficient use of human resources. The power this gave to states, and to adults operating for reasons of state, could be used for or against children's interests. The being/becoming distinction, and the happy fiction of the standard adult (see Chapter 1), then, together open the possibility of the *abuse* of children by giving adults power over them. It also closes off children's opportunities to protest against such abuses on their own behalf by casting doubt on their ability to know anything better than an adult. Silent dependency is a trap. How can you defend yourself from those who are supposed to protect you if part of the 'protection' they offer is to speak to the world on your behalf?

Giving children a voice?

Today, the failings of individual adults, adult institutions and states are widely recognized. It has become clear that the interests of children, adults and states do not always coincide. As we saw in Chapter 2, the global spread of the model of the developmental state has been accompanied by an increasing awareness of that potential difference of interests and of the scope for the abuse of children that is opened by adult's power over them. The UN Convention on the Rights of the Child (General Assembly of the UN 1989) is, among other things, an attempt to address this problem. When children are caught within places and spaces defined by abusive adults, institutions or states, the figure of the 'global child citizen' promises a place 'outside', a place in international law from which children can speak independently. It recognizes children's voices and promises children a chance to have a voice of their own.

Making an 'outside' place for children in which and from which they can speak for themselves is no simple matter. It may be obvious that the power structure of the developmental state allows for abuse and exploitation, and that children are sometimes the only people who know about it. Children's need for voices of their own to defend themselves against adult's power may also be clear. But the intellectual legacy of the dominant framework continues to suggest that 'voices' belong only to human beings, while the powerful institutional legacy of the developmental state continues to present children as human becomings. There is, then, a marked tension between the need for children to speak and to be heard, and the traditional view that only adults are worth listening to.

We shall shortly turn to an examination of the changing position of child witnesses in criminal courts in England and Wales. We shall see that new physical places – video-interview rooms – are being made for children to speak from. But first we need to know more about the difficulties of changing children's place at the level of international law and global regulation. We need to take a close look at the UN Convention on the Rights of the Child (General Assembly of the UN 1989).

The promise of a 'global place' for children

The UN Convention on the Rights of the Child was adopted by the General Assembly of the UN in 1989. It comprises 54 separate Articles, most of which cover some aspect of children's lives, such as adoption, education, health or military service. At the time of writing, all countries, save the USA, have ratified the Convention. For a state to ratify the Convention is effectively for that state to make a promise to observe each of the 54 Articles. What sort of promises are these?

Article 6 is a recognition of every child's inherent right to life, and a commitment to ensuring, to the maximum extent possible, the survival and development of every child under a given state's authority. Article 19 is a promise to take all appropriate measures to protect children from violence, injury, abuse and neglect. Article 24 is a promise to aim at providing children with the highest possible levels of health. Article 28 assures children the right to an education. These Articles are no more than the promises we could expect any country that aspires to the model of the developmental state to make to itself. They are about preserving and investing in children.

The Convention also recognizes, however, that the reasons and ambitions of state can come into conflict with children's interests. Thus, Article 38 makes the modest, but sadly necessary, commitment that children under 15 should not be recruited into a state's armed forces. In case children are identified by a state as a useful source of cheap labour, Article 31 recognizes children's rights to rest and leisure, and Article 32 provides for regulation of, and limitations to, children's employment. In view of many states' histories of persecuting ethnic, religious and/or linguistic minorities in the interest of narrow nationalism, Article 30 provides that each child should be able to enjoy their own culture, to practise their own religion and to speak their own language.

The interlocking Articles of the Convention offer children an internationally recognized set of rights that they can hold in independence of the interests and activities of the adults that directly surround them. The Convention, then, offers a 'place', albeit a virtual one consisting of promises, outside of the physical and cultural space they occupy. It is a 'place' in which children as 'global citizens' may find means to make their state protect them properly, or, if they are under attack from their own state, a means to seek protection from external sources. The place of the Convention is a peculiar 'global place'. It is part of the geographical world of state boundaries and governmental responsibility, yet it cannot be found in any single location. It is big enough to encompass all states and all children, yet it cannot be grasped outside the documents and arguments of international law and international agreement. The 'time' of the Convention is also unusual. It provides for all of today's and tomorrow's children, but, being a set of promises, can provide these children, as yet, only with an imagined future. We might well be sceptical of the practical value of such a 'place'. It seems to have all the features of a Utopia – literally, a 'no-where'. At least one author (King 1997) sees the virtual and promissory nature of the 'place' that the Convention offers children as reason to doubt whether it will ever yield real, significant benefits for them. But promises, however virtual or abstract they are, are not 'nothings'. So what mechanisms exist to hold states to the promises they have made?

Article 44 is an undertaking on the part of signatory states to submit five-yearly reports on their progress toward implementing the Convention to the United Nations Committee on the Rights of the Child (UNCRC), and to make these reports widely available to the public. Article 45 allows for the United Nations Children's Fund (Unicef), or any other appropriate expert body, to provide states with advice on how to implement the Convention and to make reports on implementation to the UNCRC. In other words, states are to be encouraged to fulfil their promises by the possibility of embarrassing exposure of their failures to do so by the Unicef or by any interested members of the public. The Convention ultimately relies for any force that it has on its perceived legitimacy, on the moral obligations and sentiments that surround promises, and on pressures exerted on states by public opinion and lobbying organizations. Now that we have found out what sort of document the Convention is, we can ask what promises it makes about the recognition of children's voices.

Global principles: particular exceptions

Article 12 contains the Convention's provision for children's voices. It reads as follows:

Article 12
1 States Parties shall assure to the child who is capable of forming his or her own views the right to express those views freely in all matters affecting the child, the views of the child being given due weight in accordance with the age and maturity of the child.
2 For this purpose, the child shall in particular be provided the opportunity to be heard in any judicial and administrative proceedings affecting the child, either directly, or through a representative or an appropriate body, in a manner consistent with the procedural rules of national law.

(General Assembly of the UN 1989)

Article 12 advances a principle about children's participation within the state's decision-making processes. The states that have ratified the Convention have promised to recognize children's ability to speak for themselves, to make efforts to hear what they say and to give 'weight' to their views. In effect, the Article recognizes that children may have something important to say that adults do not already know. In this respect, it works against the assumption that it is always possible or preferable for adults to speak for children. So, the Article acknowledges that adults cannot always be relied upon to speak on children's behalf, and that adults' interests do not always coincide with those of children. It promises a 'place' for children that is outside the cocoons of preservation and mediation that surround them when they are defined as human becomings. It would seem, in this respect, to allow for the recognition of children as human beings. Plenty of scope, however, is left for deviation from these principles. The promise has been made under quite specific terms. It applies only to those children who are deemed 'capable of forming' (General Assembly of the UN 1989) their own views. Even those children who are deemed 'capable' cannot expect to be heard clearly and simply as speaking for themselves. Their 'age and maturity' (General Assembly of the UN 1989) will modify the 'weight' or significance that is subsequently given to what they say. The Article, then, is *ambivalent* about children, about their capabilities to have voices of their own, and about the level of attention that should be given to those voices.

Even as it recognizes the possibility of children speaking for themselves, the Article also generates and contains a form of childhood ambiguity. Though we might expect the Convention, as a global ruling on children's rights, to resolve the issues surrounding children's voices, instead it houses a contradiction between views of children as adult's moral equals and views of children as minor and inferior. It does not tell us whether children are human beings or human becomings, rather it is built on the contradiction between these two distinct views of children. How are we to account for this contradiction within the Convention and for the ambiguity around the issue of children's voice that it carries?

A close reading of Article 12 reveals that its promises have been very carefully crafted. These promises can be fulfilled by a very wide range of different responses to the matter of children's voices. At one end of the range, the view could be taken that since all political decisions covering domestic and foreign policy have the potential to 'affect' the child, children should be allowed to vote in democratic elections. Alternatively however, the Article could be read as a promise to hear children only on matters that affect them more directly, on matters of adoption, say, or of the distribution of caregiving between divorcing parents. The Article allows children to speak for themselves on the condition that they are capable of forming their own views, but does not spell out who is to decide whether children have this capability. It promises that weight will be given to children's words, but who is to decide how much weight should be given and at what levels of age and maturity?

Given the breadth of possible interpretations of Article 12, and the breadth of understandings and treatments of children that it allows for, it would be easy to conclude that the Article is so ambivalent and so widely drawn that it promises nothing at all. We might feel that it has been swamped by its own ambivalence about childhood or, that the burden of childhood ambiguity has made it practically ineffective as a piece of global regulation. But if we think a little further about the nature of the Convention as a set of promises, we shall see that Article 12 could scarcely be anything *but* ambivalent about childhood.

As we have seen, the Convention makes promises about the future of the world's children. The biggest promise it makes is that the Articles it contains will be applicable in practice to *all* the world's children, wherever they live and whatever the general condition of childhood in their country. In order to provide for each and every child, however, its provisions must be seen to be capable of covering the case of each *particular* child. Abstract principles are all very well, but unless those principles can be seen as practically applicable in the case of each child in particular, they would amount to nothing but empty promises. The authors of Article 12, then, had to find a way to make the *general* and the *particular* meet each other on the page. If Article 12 did not produce general principles it could not properly count as a piece of *global* regulation. But if the Article did not also allow for specificities and particularities of children's lives, even those that might involve the relaxation or obviation of its general principles, it would not appear to be applicable in the *particular* cases of each and every child, and would, therefore, ultimately be an empty promise. However strongly the authors of the Article may have been convinced of the need to recognize children as speakers in their own right, they had to face up to and deal with the possibility that particular children, say the very young, might well have limited capabilities. If the Article had not taken this possibility into account, then some states would have been able to declare it entirely impractical on the grounds of its failure to allow for those specificities. It could be dismissed as being too general or abstract. In order to be taken seriously as a piece of global regulation then, in order to avoid being dismissed as either too narrow in focus or as too abstract to be useful, Article 12 had to contain ambiguity over children's status as human beings or human becomings.

If the Convention is about promising to make a new place for children, a place in which they can speak and be heard independently of adults, then our brief examination of Article 12 indicates that this is a very complicated task. This complexity arises because the Convention relies for any force it might have on its moral status as a promise that should be kept by all the states that have ratified it. Simply to declare that all the world's children are human beings would have been an empty promise since the practicality and thus legitimacy of such a general declaration could easily have been challenged. Perhaps this is why the Convention's title reads 'on the Rights of the Child' rather than 'of the Rights of the Child'.

Distributing childhood ambiguity

We can see that the Convention does not amount to a clear declaration that children are human beings rather than human becomings. Instead it has involved the production of a form of childhood ambiguity, an ambiguity that could not be avoided if the global promise was to be one that was both worth keeping and possible to hold states to. One question about the Convention remains outstanding, however. We might expect a piece of global regulation like the Convention to be crystal clear in its terms and provisions. The less clear it is and the more ambivalent, surely the less of a 'convention' or agreement it could be? Article 12 in particular carries a heavy burden of childhood ambiguity. Even if this ambiguity is an inevitable result of the promissory nature of the Convention, as we have argued, doesn't the burden of this ambiguity, concentrated so densely within Article 12, threaten the legitimacy of the Convention?

If the Convention had been intended to clarify children's position all at once, it would indeed crumple under this burden, but the Convention operates in a rather different way. Having generated childhood ambiguity, it then lays the responsibility for managing that ambiguity on the legislatures and policy-makers of the states that have ratified it. It is those states that now have to take on their own part of the burden of childhood ambiguity. The burden of ambiguity, once generated, is divided up and its resolution is deferred. This is actually quite an effective way of giving states the task and responsibility of thinking seriously about children's voices. The problem of silent dependency, once experienced by children alone, now belongs in part to states as well. So Article 12 is a way of raising the awareness of the problems of children's silencing and ensuring that states agree to own their share of that problem.

Promising improvement

The Convention, like other 'global' features of the age of uncertainty, is generating childhood ambiguity. Unlike the ambiguity that surrounds children 'out of place', however, the burden of this regulatory ambiguity does not come to rest solely on children's shoulders. As childhood becomes more ambiguous, as neither the traditional terms of being nor becoming are suitable to describe the conditions of their lives, we might think that the grounds for changing children's lives for the better are vanishing. If they are not clearly becomings, then they cannot be protected, while if they are not clearly beings they cannot be respected. As our brief examination of Article 12 shows, however, the possibilities for making children's lives better are not disappearing in the age of uncertainty. Rather the kinds of understanding of childhood that we need to have in order to develop such interventions is changing. Clear definitions of children either as human becomings or as human beings are unlikely to tell us how to go about improving children's circumstances in contemporary societies. Ambiguity, once created, cannot be wished away. But the burden of childhood's ambiguity can be distributed in different ways with different outcomes for children. The burden can be placed on children alone, or shared by children, adults and adult institutions. Bearing this in mind, we can now turn to our second example of 'places' for children's speech – UK criminal courts.

Child witnesses in adult courts

Witnesses, and the accounts they give, are a vital element of the prosecution of criminal offences in the UK and in most other jurisdictions. The witness is a person who is deemed to have privileged access to information that bears on the guilt or innocence of the accused. Their role in the courtroom is to tell the court in their own words what they have seen or what they know of the circumstances surrounding the alleged offence. In the UK they also have to answer questions designed to test the credibility of the account they have given. This is called 'cross-examination'. The courtroom is a place in which one's ability to speak accurately of the past and give account of one's knowledge has a crucial bearing on decision-making. Because speech is so important in court, witnesses must be able to satisfy the court that they are at least capable of speaking for themselves and of doing so accurately. If it could not be assumed that witnesses are at least capable of telling the truth as they saw it, then there would be very little sense in hearing what they have to say or in testing its credibility. The basic functions of the courtroom require speakers of a very particular kind. As Walker Perry and Wrightsman (1991) have it:

> In order to be allowed to testify, the courts insist that any potential witness must possess certain characteristics. These include the capacity to observe, sufficient intelligence and adequate memory to store information, the ability to communicate, an awareness of the difference between truth and falsehood and an appreciation of the obligation to speak truthfully.
>
> (Walker Perry and Wrightsman 1991: 37)

So if one is to take the role of the witness, one must be deemed to possess the faculties that would allow one to stand as an accurate record of past events, to be able to communicate that record, and to be aware of the sanctions that one may suffer if one gave corrupt testimony. A witness must possess all these faculties if they are to be able to speak in court, safe in the assurance that the court will at least attend to their words. Each of these faculties helps to guarantee the capacity of the witness to speak independently. This 'independence' of speech is vital because witnesses' usefulness in the court rests on their unique possession of information that bears on the guilt or innocence of the accused.

While it is normally assumed that adults have all these vital faculties and that they are thus capable of speaking for themselves, a question mark has traditionally hung over children. The reasons for this should be obvious. As we saw earlier, within the dominant framework, children are understood as being incapable of speaking *for themselves*. Children's relative lack of socialization means that they are speaking from a position of ignorance of social conventions and roles. If they do not understand social roles in general, how are they then to understand the obligations and expectations of being a witness? If they are unaware of social conventions, how are they then to comprehend the importance of telling the truth, or to understand the sanctions that might be imposed on them if they do not tell the truth? The problems that surround child witnesses run even deeper when we consider Piaget's (1955) views. If children are at a distance from rationality and from a full and accurate comprehension of the world and of their place in it, can they be said to have the capacity to give an accurate account of past events? Because children are understood to be at some distance from journey's end and from the standard adulthood by which the court judges the quality of its witnesses, courts have traditionally had difficulty in hearing children's testimony. Each child witness is preceded into court by the question of whether they really belong there. Each child witness cuts an ambiguous figure in the courtroom.

Competence tests

It takes only a little imagination to see the significance of this perceived inability of children to speak for themselves. Let us say that a child was the only witness to a criminal assault on their person by an adult. Imagine that this assault had taken place within a relationship of dependency, with all that implies for the silencing of children. If such a case as this were brought before a court, the child would be at once the most important witness *and* the person least qualified to testify. In a case like this, the silencing of children that can accompany their dependency would tend to be reinforced by the conditions of the normal operation of courts. Further, since courts require witnesses to speak for themselves, no one else would be acceptable as a witness on the child's behalf. How, then, is the child's testimony to be heard?

The problem for courts and for child witnesses is not that it is certain that children lack the faculties necessary to 'speak for oneself'. After all, the division between human being and human becoming is commonly understood to be crossed somehow by children as they get older. Some children may be further along the journey to adulthood than others. Thus children's spoken testimony is not simply excluded in all cases from court proceedings. Rather, each potential child witness is placed in the position of having to demonstrate their level of competence so that the court may decide whether they are worth hearing or not. Child witnesses bear the burden of the ambiguity of their status and the ambiguity of their belonging in court.

To address this problem, children have historically been presented with 'competence tests' (Pigot *et al.* 1989; Walker Perry and Wrightsman 1991). Their performance in competence tests is the basis of the court's decision as to whether to let them stand as witness. These tests, usually brief conversations between judge and child, have varied in nature in the UK from questions that attempt to determine whether the child knows the difference between right and wrong or truth and falsehood, to the judge's decisions about whether a child's testimony is 'understandable' or not (Criminal Justice Act 1991: Home office 1991). If the child passes the test, then their evidence is deemed admissible. But even after the completion of a competence test to the satisfaction of legal procedure, child witnesses must continue to demonstrate, for the sake of the jury, that they are mature enough to be taken seriously. Thus, the child witness in a traditional UK courtroom setting had, simultaneously, to provide information to influence two distinct decisions being made by the jury:

- Is the account the witness offers credible?
- Is the witness in a position to offer a credible account?

When children are the sole bearers of the burden of ambiguity they are therefore placed in a similar position to those 'expert witnesses' (Smith and

Wynne 1989) such as medics, psychologists, accountants and forensic scientists, who appear before court as knowledgeable professionals, and who have to establish that they are indeed knowledgeable enough for their account to be heard and taken seriously. Satisfying these two agendas at once is difficult enough for a trained and experienced expert witness. In so far as a child is aware of this double agenda, being a carrier of ambiguity may undermine their confidence, make their appearance in court extremely stressful and therefore lead to a poor and unconvincing performance as a witness. This has made it difficult for children, even those capable of articulate speech and who have passed competence tests, to be effective witnesses in courtrooms in the UK (Pigot *et al.* 1989). But, as we shall now see, childhood ambiguity is currently being redistributed in courts in England and Wales by the creation of a new kind of place in which and from which child witnesses can speak.

Video-recorded testimony and the distribution of ambiguity

The peculiar problems facing child witnesses were recognized in the UK in the late 1980s. Increasing awareness of child sexual abuse throughout the 1980s had sharpened the issue considerably. By 1989, an advisory group had published a report on a possible solution – the use of video-recording technology to tape interviews with children for later presentation in court as their testimony (Pigot *et al.* 1989). The Criminal Justice Act 1991 made such use of video-technology admissible in court, and in 1992 the *Memorandum of Good Practice on Video-Recorded Interviews with Child Witnesses for Criminal Proceedings* (Home Office and Department of Health 1992) was published. It contained detailed guidance on precisely how to conduct and record such interviews. These interviews are carried out by joint investigative teams comprising one social worker and one police officer. They are conducted in rooms specially constructed for this purpose in accordance with the standards set out in the *Memorandum* (Home Office and Department of Health 1992). A videotape is made of the interview so that it can be played back in court at a later date in the place of important parts of the child's testimony. How, then, can the use of video-interviews help child witnesses to speak for themselves?

We have seen how standard courtroom assumptions, expectations and practices place a burden of ambiguity on the child witness. Courts' uncertainty over children's reliability as witnesses becomes focused on and carried by the child. The burden of ambiguity takes the form of the child having to address their performance as a witness to two questions at once. They have to establish *both* that their account of past events is credible *and* that they are mature enough to offer a credible account of past events. The contemporary use of video has a distinctive feature that helps to redistribute the burden. In the traditional courtroom the child witness had to perform as witness at the same time as that performance was observed. But with a video-record, the child's performance as witness and the presentation of that performance to the court are separated in time. This removes the double agenda from the moment at which the child speaks. This means that as the child witnesses speak for the video-record, they are under no obligation to demonstrate that they are mature enough to offer a credible account of past events. The burden of that decision now falls squarely on judge and jury. Further, with the use of video-recording, the words of the child witness are uttered in a context where their fitness to testify is not an issue. Police and social work interview teams, unlike juries, are not charged with the responsibility of deciding whether child witnesses and their accounts are credible. Instead, they are simply gathering evidence.

The video-suite where interviews are recorded is a place in which normal considerations of whether children fit 'standard adulthood' or not do not apply. It is a place in which children can speak for themselves because it is a place that excludes questions of their ignorance or unreason. It defers those questions till later. Court personnel, of course, may still raise these questions. Indeed video-evidence is admissible in court only if the child witness is also prepared to be cross-examined (Lee 1999). But the initial and, perhaps most difficult hurdle that confronts child witnesses, the fundamental issue of their status as becomings or beings, has been removed from one of the places at which they speak.

Conclusion

In this chapter we have seen that childhood ambiguity is being recognized as a problem both at the levels of global regulation and in the details of decision-making in UK courts of law. The problems that this ambiguity generates for children are being addressed by the creation both of a virtual, promissory place in which and from which they can speak for themselves (the UN Convention) and, in England and Wales at least, by the creation of real places in which and from which they can speak for themselves. In this sense then, the age of uncertainty is offering children a degree of 'recognition' that has been denied them in previous years. The 'new places' for children's speech may, like the UN Convention, always be in the position of having to prove their worth or may, like video-witnessing, be very limited and partial in the effects they produce. They are significant developments none the less since unlike previous strategies for dealing with children, they do not depend on a clear decision over children's status, but instead work with and through childhood's ambiguity.

Throughout our argument so far, we have seen how policies and practices devised for children by adults have often rested on certain understandings of what children are. The early developmental state understood them as investments to be cultivated and protected. The dominant framework understood them as vulnerable becomings. So what understandings of children are the new places for children being built? The 'recognition' that they offer is not based on a new, clear conception of children as beings.

Neither is it based on any certainty that they are human becomings. Neither Article 12 nor video-interviewing practices pretend to resolve children's ambiguous status. Instead, in both of our examples, we saw that this ambiguity is being broken up, deferred and shared. Childhood ambiguity is being put in circulation among the state's policy-makers, and among court personnel not so that it can be ignored or resolved, but so that it does not come to rest solely on the shoulders of children.

Now that we have reached the end of this section, you may have noticed that many of the examples we have examined have involved media technologies. Television, ICT and video-recorders have all had starring roles. In some cases we have argued that they have helped to generate childhood ambiguity. In others we have argued that they are helping to manage childhood ambiguity. We have focused so closely on media technologies because such technologies are able to change the nature of 'place'. Children, as we have seen, are often understood to have 'proper' places. Some of these proper places are obviously physical and concrete. Some of these proper places seem more symbolic and cultural, for example children's place in hierarchies of age and power. Both the physical and cultural placement of children, has long gone hand-in-hand with the understanding of children as becomings. Conceptions of children and childhood have both supported and been supported by their physical and cultural placement and regulation. Television, however, has changed the family home, ICT is changing the classroom and video is changing courtrooms. The being/becoming distinction is being blurred just as those places are being changed. The age of uncertainty, as it bears on children, is as much about the use of technology changing 'place' as it is about responses to global economic relationships increasing our uncertainty about the future.

◯ PART THREE

Human becomings and social research

◯───────────────────────────────

In Part one we saw how the being/becoming division developed over the centuries and came to dominate our thinking about children and about growing up. Part one and Part two together illustrated how this division is becoming less useful as a means of describing and understanding the lives of children and adults. Adulthood can no longer be assumed to be stable and complete. Childhoods are becoming increasingly ambiguous. This presents us with a problem. How are we to think about growing up, to study childhoods and relations between adults and children, when the terms that have been so helpful in the past no longer apply?

We could retreat from the social study of childhood entirely, despairing at the lack of viable basic concepts. Alternatively, we could ignore the difficulties that now attend attempts to define 'being', forget what we have learned about the close relationship between human being and standard adulthood, and continue the recent trend to abandon the category 'human becoming' along with the dominant framework. This would leave us with plenty of respect for children as beings in their own right, but would also limit our ability to take growing up seriously as a source of questions and possibilities.

But we have a third option. We can search for new concepts and terms with which to organize our thinking about childhood. We can look for understandings of human life that avoid the problems that now surround both human being and human becoming as we have understood them so far. Rather than abandon human becoming to portray all humans, regardless of age, as complete and independent, we might instead develop concepts that allow us to see all humans, adults and children alike, as fundamentally dependent and incomplete. In other words, we can try to 'multiply' becoming beyond the limits that the dominant framework, the developmental state and the figure of the standard adult have together set around it.

In Chapter 7 we shall explore some views of the human that have never depended on the figure of the standard adult, views that have always understood this figure, with its independence, self-control and self-possession, as an exaggeration and an oversimplification. We shall see that the 'supplementation' that the dominant framework saw as a task that could be begun in youth and finished at adulthood, actually never comes to an end. We shall see that rather than possessing themselves, humans, regardless of age, 'borrow' from their surroundings to make themselves what they are. These views make of human life an endless and endlessly variable process of becoming.

But just to advance this view is not enough to make a difference to the way that childhood is thought. So in Chapter 8 we shall describe how it may change the bases on which the sociology of childhood is practised, how it may change our understanding of the three key concepts of agency, convention and ethics. In Chapter 9, by way of conclusion, we shall return to the issue of 'growing up' to offer a broader way of understanding it than is available within the dominant framework.

7

Childhood and extension: the multiplication of becoming

We saw in Chapter 1 how the major characteristics of children have been drawn in opposition to those that adults are understood to possess. The child has been seen as lacking the wholeness, the fullness, and stable self-possession that adults enjoy. This being/becoming division underlies and informs relationships between adults and children. It provides adults both with powers over children and with the right and obligation to mediate for them and to protect them. The relationship between being and becoming is clearly a very important issue for students of childhood because, in the case of adults and children, power follows being.

But this question of being and becoming has also been central to philosophical argument for millennia. The relationship between stability and change, between fixed properties and processes, has been a perennial philosophical problem, visited and revisited over the centuries. Philosophers as varied in approach and intent as Whitehead (1929); Hegel (1991); Plato (1994) and Spinoza (1994) have argued about the basic nature of the world in terms that resemble our being/becoming division. Sometimes, things that change or 'become', and thus give a hint of instability, have been treated as inferior or illusory, as the deceptive surface manifestation of a more fundamental set of stabilities (Plato 1994). Sometimes it is the idea of 'being' as independent stability that has been criticized, critics preferring to see apparent stabilities as the passing effects of more fundamental flux and change (Whitehead 1929).

The relationship between being and becoming has not just been a concern of philosophers. The contrast between being and becoming has also often provided the bases for cultural and political struggle. The being/becoming division is one of the resources available to us to think through the rights and wrongs of social order and social control. Think of the contrasts that can be drawn between societies regulated through the unchanging authority of royal families or religious doctrine, and those based on democracy, a political system that claims to respond to the changing preferences and decisions of the populace. Consider the personal qualities we look for in our leaders; often, certainty of purpose and unchanging commitment to principles; sometimes, openness to alternatives, to discussion and to new information that may change their minds.

Among the strongest indications of the link between being and becoming and general issues of control and social order are the rights and privileges given to people along with the recognition that they are beings, the privileges and powers that adults, for example, have over children. As long as they are seen as independent in their stability, adults can qualify as needing, in principle, no external control. Beings can self-regulate and should therefore be free. In contrast, wherever children have been seen as dependent in their instability, they have also been understood as in need of external control. Sociologists of childhood, in seeking recognition for children as beings, have been participants in a political and cultural struggle, working in the hope that the more children can be seen as beings, the more access they will have to the privileges and powers of self-determination. We have seen, however, just how problematic the terms of this struggle have become. The dissolution of economic supports of standard adulthood and the growing ambiguities of childhood that we are witnessing in our age of uncertainty together suggest that new terms are needed.

Given the depth of philosophical concern with the basic question of being and becoming, it would be rather surprising if the view arrived at in the mid-twentieth century, the view of being and becoming as opposites, one full, complete, stable and independent, the other incomplete, unstable and dependent, was the only view available. In this chapter we will suggest that as students of childhood, our options are broader than this. We are going to develop sensitizing concepts that are fit for the study of contemporary childhoods by taking heed of recent philosophical approaches to issues of completeness, incompleteness, being and becoming. We will argue that adults, like children, are incomplete, that they are dependent on 'extensions' and 'supplements' for their powers and abilities. We will also argue that many different states of becoming need to be recognized. First, however, we need to understand a little of the social and political context in which our alternative view of completeness, incompleteness and becoming developed. This will take us back in time to the years following the Second World War.

The critique of central control

Europe and the USA fared differently in the Second World War. The USA had been spared the extensive damage to infrastructure that European states suffered and the mass production of weaponry had even boosted its economy. At the close of hostilities, the USA was in a position to secure western Europe as a future market for its goods and as a future trading partner. To this end the USA extended reconstruction loans to western European governments. In some cases these loans would help rebuild industrial infrastructure (UK and Germany). In other cases they would help states to industrialize on Fordist lines for the first time (France and Italy). The Marshall Plan for European reconstruction was also designed to ward off the potential for communist revolution in fragile western European societies, by laying the grounds for economic and political stability (Tavor Bannet 1989).

Alongside the construction or reconstruction of an industrial base, it was also necessary to rehouse workers and to provide them with the degree of security that would allow them to consume the new volumes of mass-produced goods. Post-war reconstruction, then, involved many western European governments in long-term planning for the coordination of the needs of their populations with the needs of industry. So one of the effects of post-war reconstruction was an increase in the extent to which western European societies were centrally planned. These changes were particularly dramatic in France. With the assistance of the Marshall Plan, France was converted from a predominantly agricultural society to a predominantly Fordist industrial society over the brief period of 20 years (Tavor Bannett 1989). In this period of rapid change, following hard on Nazi occupation during the war, it was easy for French intellectuals of the political left to see this US-sponsored increase in the central control of society as a new form of the totalitarianism that had only recently been defeated. Strong central government with a clear national industrial plan, giving each citizen a function in and responsibility to their state was, for some, too close to Nazism for comfort. Much of the thinking of the post-war political left thus became critical of centralized authority. Anything resembling 'hierarchical structures of authority and domination, standardisation, systematisation [or] programmed conformities' (Tavor Bannett 1989: 232) became open to attack.

In this intellectual atmosphere it became possible not only to criticize the French state by highlighting any resemblances it had to a totalitarian regime, but also to question existing political authority at its very roots. The Fordist solution offered security and stability to society as long as central planning and coordination of industry and population could be maintained. The promise of Fordist reconstruction was that the more complete the plan, the tighter regulated and coordinated society became, the more stable and prosperous it would be. Central control, the tighter and more extensive the better, was equated with stability. Some authors, however (Derrida 1967; Deleuze and Guattari 1972, 1980) worked to question the very possibility of complete stability and coordination, and to challenge the reassurances that the equation between central control and stability offered. The aim of these authors was not only to resist the existing stabilities, but also to make the general promise of stability through central control ring hollow. Working toward this aim meant broadening their focus from the realities of French society to a fundamental re-examination of notions of completeness and incompleteness. Our first source, Derrida (1976), raised the question about the possibility of 'completion' in general. We will be using his arguments to question the completeness of human being.

Derrida and incompleteness

For Derrida (1976), the equation between central control and stability did not necessarily hold good, yet he was well aware that this equation had long informed the distribution of power within western culture. Only those deemed capable of controlling themselves from their own 'centres' have enjoyed the benefits of being thought stable and reliable. It is no accident that powerless groups throughout history, such as women, slaves and children, have also been conceived of as being *unable* to control themselves. Wherever we find a powerless group, we also find the idea that a state of powerlessness is appropriate to them because of their deficiencies. In contrast, those who have been deemed capable of self-control have been understood as having this capability by virtue of the quality of 'self-presence' (Derrida 1976; Gasché 1994).

The quality of self-presence is rather mysterious. It mixes up matters of economic self-ownership and the ownership of others (such as slaves, wives and children) with attributions of certain personal characteristics like consistency and trustworthiness. For Derrida (1976), the most interesting manifestation of this notion of self-presence is to be found in questions of voice and of the ownership of one's voice. Self-present persons are deemed to have the ability to control their own utterances so that they always intend to mean what they say. When adults bear witness in court (see Chapter 6), for example, they are assumed to possess self-presence to be capable of meaning what they say. In court self-presence is not treated as a guarantee of honesty but provides a standard against which honesty can be tested.

The voice of the self-present person is clear and its meaning is easily understood by other self-present persons, because they can rest assured that the speaker is speaking his (*sic*) mind and taking full responsibility for what he says. Self-present persons, then, are trustworthy. Their voices and opinions are to be taken seriously simply because, having spoken with full control over their words, they are unlikely later to declare that they did not mean what they said. The self-present, then, are deemed to own their own voices, to control their utterances from their own centre of self-awareness and so to be stable and reliable. Self-presence, then, is another way of saying 'human being'. It is on the basis of self-ownership, self-control and trustworthiness that a community of the self-present can form and exclude those who do not 'own' themselves. The voices of women, children and slaves have historically been muted, partly because they were not deemed to have voices of their own that were worth listening to. As we have seen in the case of children and the law (see Chapter 6), the effects of the notion of self-presence are still with us today.

The paradox of power and completion

Thus far we have examined self-presence as an ideology, a set of ideas that has sustained the differences in power between property-owning adult men and the dispossessed since ancient Greece (Derrida 1997). If we feel angry about this state of affairs, as well we might, we could decide that the ideology of self-presence is mere prejudice, the result of a nasty conspiracy of the powerful against the weak. We could argue that the dispossessed do, or at least should, have ownership of themselves, that they are in fact just as self-present as any property-owning adult man. We could seek to broaden the category of 'human being' to include all humans, and return voice and self-possession to those from whom it has been stolen. But Derrida (1976) takes a rather different path.

Derrida (1976) does not argue that everyone does, or should, enjoy the privileges that go along with living out the equation between central control and stability that we find in self-presence. Rather, his concern is to make that equation ring hollow by arguing that the mysterious quality of self-presence cannot be understood simply as a stable possession, and that even those whose power rests on the quality of self-presence cannot properly be said to possess it. To make this case, Derrida (1976) focuses on anxieties that have attended the mediation of voice over the millennia, paying particular attention to the medium of 'writing'.

Derrida's (1976) work reveals that over the years many philosophers and thinkers have felt that there is something 'dangerous' about writing. Where does this peculiar sense of danger come from? As we have seen, the ability of speakers to mean what they say is fundamental to their trustworthiness. Because self-present speakers are taken to mean what they say, 'voice' is very vehicle of their power. But what if the powerful wanted their words to carry over distance and time? What if face-to-face communication was not enough to get one's orders carried out? Under these conditions one's own voice alone is not sufficient. It is in need of supplementation and extension. To make their power useful and to establish their control over others, the powerful would need to rely upon others to convey their words across space, or to remember their words over time.

Supplementation of the voice, however, breaks self-presence. How can a messenger be as strong a guarantee of trustworthy stability as the author of the message? After all, a messenger might not remember the message properly. The messenger might even deliberately change the message, committing the original speaker to words they did not mean. In the absence of the author of the message, there is no way of establishing its accuracy. The same problems apply to the written word as a supplement of speech. It is not speech, but rather stands for, supplements and extends speech. As the messenger of speech, writing breaks the relationship of self-presence on which the mutual trust of the powerful and the exclusion of the dispossessed depend. This is what makes writing a 'dangerous supplement' (Derrida 1976: 141). If the powerful are to use their power to affect the world around them by sending messages, to issue instructions or to communicate their desires, views and opinions, they have no choice but to use such media as other persons or writing, to supplement their speech. But these other supplementary media necessarily erode the conditions on which their power is based. Media other than speech are threatening because they cannot convey the full sense of self-presence, the full sense of the speaker's complete self-ownership and self-control. Without them, however, the power of the powerful cannot be exercised.

In the complex of anxieties that Derrida (1976) discovers, mediation, extension and supplementation *in general* are understood as dangerous. The nature of the danger is clear. Extension and supplementation expose the necessary dependency of those whose good character and power is based on their claim to self-present independence, to personal, central control and autonomy. Derrida (1976) tells us, then, that the power and self-possession of the powerful is never complete. As soon as their spoken word is conveyed, they are distanced from themselves, dispossessed of themselves in the moment that self-possession is broken. The equation of central control and stability rings hollow, because even the most independent and powerful are made incomplete, distanced from their self-presence, in their bids to exercise their power.

Extension and supplementation are certainly dangerous from the perspective of the powerful, but things look quite different from the perspective of the powerless. Those who have already been denied self-presence, such as slaves, women and children, have little to fear from Derrida's (1976) paradox of completion. If they have already been taken to lack self-presence then supplementation, mediation and extension, along with the dependency they imply, are just 'business as usual' for them. While the powerful may fear supplementation and mediation in general, the powerless are more likely to be concerned only with the *quality* of specific situations in which they are mediated or supplemented; some extensions are helpful, some supplementations useful, others damaging.

Nature, culture and supplementation

So far we have seen how Derrida's (1976) work reveals the dependency and incompleteness of those whose power rests on images of independent completeness and stability. We have seen that rather than redescribe the dispossessed as self-present beings, on the model of the powerful, Derrida (1976) instead exposes limits to the possibility of self-present being. He is trying to disrupt such hierarchies as those between men and women, slaves and owners, and adults and children, by showing that the simultaneous possession and use of self-presence is impossible. For Derrida (1976), it is not that everyone, contrary to ideology, does possess or should possess self-presence, it is rather that as soon as self-presence engages with the world through media other than face-to-face conversation – in other words, as soon as it is turned to use – it becomes impossible to sustain.

These are interesting observations and they clearly have some bearing on the relative social positions of children and adults. If children have been excluded from 'voice', ignored or silenced, then this exclusion has been on the basis of an assumption that as incomplete human becomings they are not worth hearing because they are in need of supplementation either in the forms of development and socialization or in the form of an adult to speak on their behalf. Derrida's (1976) arguments would suggest, however, that *no one* can reach the standards of completeness against which this judgement is made. If we follow Derrida's (1976) arguments, the opposition of adults and children as human beings and human becomings becomes quite untenable since not even adults can qualify as human beings, if 'human being' is a state of self-present and complete independence. Adults and children, then, are not as different as the being/becoming division would suggest. Regardless of age and status, humans are dependent on mediation and supplementation. All human life is lived in extension.

These arguments certainly call the good sense of the being/becoming division into question. But it could be said that they ignore the facts of childhood incompleteness that have been assembled within the dominant framework. As we saw in Chapter 3, children are incomplete because they are more 'natural' than adults. On this view, the claim that children are especially incomplete makes perfectly good sense. Being younger, they have had less time to develop rationality or to learn society's values and expectations. The difference between adults and children, then, is as strong and certain as the difference between nature and culture. It is, in fact, the same difference.

Derrida's (1976) pursuit of themes of supplementation and incompleteness takes him to the work of Jean-Jacques Rousseau, an eighteenth-century French philosopher who wrote on many topics including education and child-rearing. There are some striking parallels between Rousseau's understandings of the relationship between nature and childhood and those we have seen in the dominant framework. For Rousseau, as for the dominant framework, nature's endowments are necessary but not sufficient to human being, and children, incomplete as they are, thus stand in need of supplementation. But, as Derrida (1976) discusses Rousseau, he poses some rather awkward questions for Rousseau that could equally well be addressed to the dominant framework. If children are incomplete by nature, then there must be such a thing as a 'natural incompleteness'. Derrida (1976: 146) asks how such a thing as a natural incompleteness could be possible. How is it that nature leaves 'gaps' in the child? Is nature in some way 'aware' that these gaps will later be filled? From what point of view does this peculiar idea of natural incompleteness make sense?

For Rousseau, a 'lack' lies with nature. Nature gives rise to unfinished products. Rousseau is ambivalent about this lack. On some occasions he is grateful for it, since it provides humanity with the ability to shape its young, to socialize them, to train them to use their powers appropriately. Incompleteness, then, allows for the development of good in the world.

On other occasions, however, Rousseau warns of the dangers that children's incomplete nature poses to humanity. Being incomplete, children
have to rely on others to extend them, and

> as soon as they can think of people as tools that they are responsible
> for activating, they use them to carry out their wishes and to supple-
> ment their own weakness. This is how they become tiresome, masterful,
> imperious, naughty and unmanageable; a development which does not
> spring from a natural love of power, but one which gives it to them.
>
> (Rousseau, cited in Derrida 1976: 147)

So from childhood incompleteness and the fact of supplementation springs
the possibility of evil. But once again we can ask from what perspective the
notion of a 'lacking' nature makes sense? From what position could such a
'lack' be seen? The following quotation gives us a clue:

> Plants are fashioned by cultivation, and men by education.
>
> (Rousseau, cited in Derrida 1976: 147)

In Rousseau, and in his natural 'lack', we are hearing the contrast between
'gamekeeping' and 'gardening' (see Chapter 2), the difference between an
understanding of nature as spontaneously plentiful and abundant and an
understanding of nature as in need of cultivation, careful pruning, weeding
and tidying. The understandings of nature as 'lacking' and of children as
naturally incomplete come to us from the dissatisfaction of gardeners, who,
finding nature's provision no longer adequate to their needs, create a mythical
relationship between an incomplete nature and completing culture. Nature's
lack and children's incompleteness derive from the great change in the
attitudes of the powerful that we described in Chapter 2.

We should also remember that 'nature', for Rousseau at least, is another
word for God. There is a theology, a particular view of God, buried in the
idea that children are incomplete. In this theology, God performs his work
of creation, then puts down his tools and departs the scene leaving human-
kind to continue his labours. Nature's 'lack' and the incompleteness of
children are a version of the Christian God's gift of 'freewill' to humanity,
the freedom of humans to sin which makes God value our virtue so highly.

Thus, Rousseau's mythic 'nature' does its work *before* the work of culture, cultivation and education, and abandons the scene *before* socialization
or development begin. If culture is the supplement of nature, then culture
and nature would seem to work at *different times*. No wonder 'growing up'
has been such a puzzle (see Chapter 1). No wonder childhood seems
to need special laws to regulate it. We have been addressing childhood
and growing up through the concepts and concerns of eighteenth-century
would-be leaders, whose ambitions led them to imagine a stark distinction
between the work of nature and the work of culture. The difference they
perceived between the time of nature's work and the time of culture's work
underlies the current distinction between complete and incomplete or being
and becoming as it is applied to 'growing up'. But if we *do not* accept the

difference between nature's time and culture's time, and if we *do* accept Derrida's (1976) arguments about the paradoxical nature of self-presence, then it is clear that supplementation and mediation are constant features of human life. On this view, adulthoods and childhoods are not to be understood as the result of the presence or absence of complete self-presence. Perhaps, then, childhoods and adulthoods could be understood as the result of differences in the patterns of supplementation, mediation and extension that surround people of different chronological ages?

Derrida (1976) offers no clear alternative to Rousseau's conception of the child. He is not concerned with producing such clear alternatives, but rather with exposing the limits to the possibility of completeness, self-control and stability. He argues that whatever independence and powers adults as human beings seem to possess arise only from the dependencies they have and from the patterns of mediation and supplementation that surround them. Derrida's deconstruction of self-presence is nevertheless an effective caution against believing in the standard model of the adult. It helps us to understand not only how it is that children are silenced or rendered powerless, but also just how shaky are those justifications of silencing and powerlessness that rest on ideas of self-presence. He has certainly drawn our attention to the ubiquity of supplements and mediation and has thus built a perspective for us from which the supposedly natural differences between completed adults and incomplete children do not look quite so credible.

In his comments on Rousseau, Derrida (1976) asks us whether we are content still to imagine nature and culture as operating in different times. Rousseau tells us that nature comes first, leaves with its work unfinished and is then replaced by the arrival of culture. Derrida (1976) asks us whether we find this general pattern convincing. But once the division between the work of nature and culture has been put in question, and once adults and children both can be seen as indebted to external supplements and mediations for whatever capabilities and powers they have, what positive descriptions of childhood can then emerge? If we cannot equate central control with stability, if we can no longer reassure ourselves with the notion that every adult contains a nugget of self-presence, wholeness and completion, what then can we say about childhood? This question takes us to our next philosophical source.

Assemblages and multiple becomings

Deleuze and Guattari (1972, 1980) wrote in the same milieu of French postwar thought as Derrida. They shared his suspicions about any equation of central control and stability. However, where Derrida tried to make this equation ring hollow, Deleuze and Guattari (1988) worked on producing a new way of describing and understanding stability and order, an account that did not depend on any core of self-control at the heart of humanity. Rather like Derrida (1976), they argued that human beings do not completely 'own' themselves, but they focused more closely on describing the 'borrowing' involved in extension and mediation. For Deleuze and Guattari (1988), stabilities and orders cannot be explained by self-presence and self-ownership, because, no matter how complete humans may seem, we constantly 'borrow' from each other, from media including speech and writing and from the powers and properties of all the world's resources, animal, vegetable and mineral. On their view, humans, regardless of age, are constitutionally unfinished. They are always indebted to someone or something else, and this indebtedness opens human life to adaptability and change.

Given the level of indebtedness of humans to their surroundings, for Deleuze and Guattari (1988) it makes little sense to talk about human beings in isolation. Much of their work attempts to persuade us to stop asking questions about fixed human nature, to stop seeing life in terms of completion, and to start thinking about 'assemblages' (Deleuze and Guattari 1988: 359). Deleuze and Guattari (1988) find their clearest illustrations of assemblages in the histories of warfare and of agriculture.

Even in the distant past of the Bronze Age, human beings were not alone on the Earth. They did not have to rely solely on their own intrinsic natures or powers. Some humans, for example, were able to extend their powers to cover geographical distance by borrowing the legs, hearts and lungs of horses. A rider on a horse is a 'man-horse' (sic) assemblage (Deleuze and Guattari 1988: 399), capable of speeds and levels of endurance that would be impossible for a human alone. In order to borrow the strength of the horse, humans first had to change the horse by capturing it and training it to follow commands. They also had to change themselves by learning about horses' habits, fears and strengths, about their food and watering needs, about the limits of horses' endurance, and by developing the skills they needed to stay mounted. As 'human' and 'horse' entered into this assemblage, then, they both changed. The borrowing of powers changed humans into 'riders' and horses into 'mounts'.

The implications of the human-horse assemblage did not stop there. They also extended into the patterns of borrowing that humans had long been involved in with metals. Humans had already extended themselves through their involvement in mining, refining and metal-working to produce tools and weapons, knives and daggers. But within a human-horse assemblage, daggers were too short to be useful for combat. The dagger was extended through further developments in metal-working into swords and lances. The basic 'human-horse' changed into the 'human-horse-sword' assemblage. But the 'human-horse' assemblage also diversified. In Deleuze and Guattari's (1988) account, where the 'human-horse' assemblage met agriculture, it made it possible to use heavier ploughs than before, to dig deeper furrows than could be dug using oxen. In this new agricultural scheme, grain surpluses could be relied upon to a greater extent than before. The 'human-horse-plough' assemblage underlay the development of the European farmer, the European city and the interdependence of the rural and the urban.

For Deleuze and Guattari (1988) each of these assemblages is a form of order, a stability that results from encounters between humans, animals and metals. In these encounters the powers and characteristics of humans, animals and metals meet each other, combine and recombine and are changed. Horses are not naturally designed as mounts, yet can be worked upon to open that possibility. The hardness and sharpness of metals is not found naturally in their ores, yet their ores can be worked upon to open the possibility of a hard, sharp edge. Humans are not naturally horse-riders, warriors or farmers, but become so through encounters with animals, metals and crop-species. Each assemblage, each order, lasts for a while, but through further encounters and possibilities, each assemblage can change and become something rather different, changing the characteristics and powers of its elements as it goes.

On this view, humans find themselves in the midst of an open-ended swirl of extensions and supplementations, changing their powers and characteristics as they pass through different assemblages. To understand the patterns of complex and open-ended becoming that humans participate in, Rousseau's discrimination between nature and culture is less than helpful. Nature never appears as a single order, complete or incomplete. Instead, we find countless potentials among humans, animals, plants and the inanimate material world, their interrelationship constantly presenting problems and possibilities. Looking through Deleuze and Guattari's (1988) eyes, we do not see a single incomplete natural order waiting to be finished by culture, we see many incomplete orderings that remain open to change. In those many different unfinished orderings, we also see many kinds of human – warriors, farmers, city dwellers – each quite different in their powers and capabilities because they each depend on and live through different sets of extensions. In short, Deleuze and Gauttari (1988) give us a picture of human life, whether adult or child, as an involvement in multiple becomings.

Assemblage, extension and childhood

These accounts may seem a very long way from issues of childhood and growing up. Yet Deleuze and Guattari (1988) have given us a framework within which to compare the various childhoods we examined in Part two. Whether children are in or out of their place, or whether new places are being made for them, we can ask what assemblages they are involved in and what extensions they are living through.

In Chapter 4, we saw that, deprived of such extensions as the four walls of a home, Brazilian street children became each other's extensions, gathering together at night for mutual protection. They made a fragile order out of the resources that were available to them. They also took up the streets as extensions, converting them from thoroughfares to an abode. It was not so much their disorderliness that made them seem threatening, but the high contrast between the ordered assemblage they made of 'child-group-street' and the assemblage that the police officers who killed them were part of an assemblage of 'police-law-state'. The children congregated in times and places that had not yet been fully incorporated into this latter assemblage, times and places where they could usually make use of the streets for their purposes in safety. Killing these children was a way for the police-law-state assemblage to prevent the emergence of an alternative order. Clearly, then, assemblages can come into conflict. We saw that the UK government is working hard to ensure that a 'parents-child-house' assemblage wins over a 'child-group-street' assemblage.

In Chapter 5 we saw how childhood ambiguity was emerging in homes and schools. These ambiguities were each the result of the incorporation of children as elements of distinct, yet overlapping assemblages. 'Parents-child-house' was a set of extensions that opened the potential for the child's dependence, while 'child-television-marketplace' arranged many of the same elements in quite a different way, opening the child to a different potential – the independence of consumer choice and 'pester-power' over parents. Similarly, elements of the 'classroom-teacher-pupil' assemblage that opened the possibility of teachers' power to direct children's becoming toward an end, are now being drawn off into another assemblage of 'person-information-computing device'. In each of these cases the child is one point of overlap of two separate assemblages. This location concentrates the difference between the assemblages on children themselves, giving rise to an effect of childhood ambiguity.

In our coverage of the UN Convention in Chapter 6, we were effectively examining the beginnings of what may become a successful new assemblage involving children. The Convention is an attempt to draw the energies and materials of states into an assemblage that protects children while not claiming complete ownership of them. Perhaps our clearest example of children in assemblage and extension is to be found in our examination of changing witnessing practices. Instead of either forgetting about or finally resolving children's ambiguity, the UK criminal justice system is using the new extension of video-recording to change the nature and powers of children as witnesses. Child witnesses' passage through court is being eased by drawing them into an assemblage of video-technologies and police and social workers.

Just as changes in patterns of extension affect the powers and characteristics of children, so they also affect the powers and characteristics, actual and perceived, of any adults involved in a changing assemblage. The teacher changes from a powerful and commanding leader to a facilitator of learning. The parent has to learn to balance the privacy of childhood within the family home with childhood's new openness to the world of consumption and mediated images. As children become fit to act as witnesses through new extensions, so the degree to which adult witnesses have always been extended by the assumption of their self-presence becomes clearer. So if we think through the terms developed by Derrida (1976) and Deleuze and Guattari (1988), we are in a position to study the powers and characteristics of both children and adults as the results of patterns of extension, patterns which themselves are open to change. We also have the germ of a way of accounting for the common relationships of power and authority between adults and children, a type of account that is an alternative to the story of the meeting of the complete and the incomplete.

As we have suggested throughout the book so far, this alternative view of human becoming is just what is called for in an age of uncertainty in which the conditions that made adulthood resemble finished human being are eroded. Ideas of assemblage and extension allow us to think of all humans alike as becomings and to give account of their powers and characteristics in terms of their dependencies. These becomings are multiple. They sometimes come into conflict with one another, especially when they share certain elements. The single becoming of the developmental state that was long identified with children and childhood, the becoming that has been presented as a clear and knowable journey with a certain end, was only ever one becoming among a much wider range. The diversity of becomings, and of human possibility, were hidden by the long-lasting stability of the order of the developmental state, an order that required children to be incomplete enough to be used as sites of investment.

Becomings, change and speed

The new terms and ideas we have introduced so far in this chapter may well prove useful in understanding changing childhoods and adulthoods as the age of uncertainty unfolds. They have certainly informed the survey of childhood that we conducted in Part two. Just as Rousseau's ideas about childhood, nature and supplementation were developed with the beginnings of the 'gardening' attitude to government, and ran alongside the emergence of the developmental state, so Derrida (1976) and Deleuze and Guattari's (1988) ideas were developed as Fordism collapsed and as what we have called the age of uncertainty began. Thinking of all humans, even adults, as incomplete becomings is certainly compatible with today's concern with flexibility, with the increasingly mediated character of society and with the tendency for the state's central control of the populations to diminish. As we multiply the term 'becoming' we prepare ourselves to understand our unknown futures as they unfold. But if these terms are to be truly useful in analysing and, perhaps, helping to change childhoods, if they are to be anything more than empty promises, we must not be tempted to use them as an excuse for ignoring existing realities. These words are not slogans to be repeated whenever we find a stable phenomenon, such as the silencing of children, that we do not agree with. To find that becomings are multiple or that all humans are fundamentally dependent on extensions, is not the end of analysis, but the beginning. One way to illustrate this is to reflect for a moment on that important question of 'nature'.

We have seen how the dominant paradigm, like Rousseau, thought of children as incomplete, because it thought of nature as incomplete and of children as in some sense natural. We have also seen how Derrida's (1976) awkward questions revealed the perspective from which these ideas made sense. It is a perspective that we might not share, since it separates nature and culture by thinking of nature as if it were a single 'person' or a God. Given this, we could rapidly come to the conclusion that any talk of childhood as 'natural' is nonsense. This would put us directly in conflict with anyone who did see 'nature' in the child. But if we are interested in persuading others of the possibilities of hearing children's voices, for example, or in playing any part in changing childhoods, to adopt such a contrary approach would be fruitless. We need to think instead of what people mean when they say 'nature', and then think again.

Very often the word 'natural' refers to anything physical or psychological concerning children. It is clear that in many physical and psychological respects, children do differ from adults. As we have already noted, children tend to be smaller than adults and they are certainly not born speaking a language. Growing up does involve physical growth and the development of language skills. But to acknowledge this is not the same as saying that children are naturally incomplete while adults are complete. It certainly does not imply that nature departs the scene early in life, leaving the work of growing up to be finished by culture.

These observations on childhood's physicality and psychology are quite in tune with Deleuze and Guattari's (1988) conception of becomings. We have already seen how their notion of assemblage involves a close relationship between human bodies and other animate and inanimate bodies. For Deleuze and Guattari (1988) anything at all can play the part of an extension and can be drawn up into an assemblage. Far from excluding any consideration of physical and psychological change, Deleuze and Guattari (1988) expand the importance of the physical beyond anything recognized by a neat division between nature and culture. Let us take the example of language. Language is among the most important human extensions. It does indeed take a while for growing children to relate themselves to it. But learning to speak is not just a matter of filling up the brain with information that nature alone could not provide. Equipped with tongue, lips, hard and soft palate, lungs and a diaphragm, we learn to speak as the muscles of these organs are shaped and developed and as we come to coordinate their movements with our nervous system, itself composed of sensory and motor neurons, the spinal cord and the brain. Learning to speak, we come to use our organs as extensions. But the learning never stops. We continue to relate to changing social life through our organs of speech. We continue to learn new words and terminologies, even whole languages, throughout life. Our physical speech organs allow us to do this. But they also provide their own obstacles. With our muscles trained to produce the sounds of one language or accent, familiar with the shapes of certain words and not others, our muscles may become strained as we practise new elements of language. It takes time for us to change our speaking habits because our speaking habits reside in the shape and strength of the tissues of our organs of speech.

As we continue using language as an extension, we can find ourselves having to speak in different settings. Speaking to more powerful people, or in front of an audience, our organs of speech may not function as we wish. We constantly have to learn and relearn how to coordinate our extensions in changing circumstances. For Deleuze and Guattari (1988), children enter the world as a combination of the very ancient (for example the pattern of lungs, trachea and vocal cords) and the very new (such as the new tissues that make up lung, trachea and vocal cords). To this extent, children are 'natural', but since the combination of old and new remains throughout life, adults are no less so.

Conclusion

Physicality and sociality, unlike Rousseau's nature and culture, take place at the same time as each other, but they are open to change at quite different speeds. Bodily organs, once devoted only to breathing and eating, came to be reorganized into a new assemblage, one capable of speech, over millions of years of evolution. Languages blend into one another or become differentiated on a scale of thousands of years. Individual words reach currency in decades; collectively shared ideas, thanks to newsprint, change by the day, and our own ideas change by the second. Just as ways of speaking lay their shape on the organs of speech, so ideas about childhood have laid their shape on the patterning of extensions and assemblages. We can change our *ideas* about children and childhood quite rapidly, but to change the *realities* must inevitably take longer because new paths of becoming have to become physical, set into patterns of extension, if they are to last any length of time or to affect any number of people.

As we advance our argument that we should 'multiply' becoming and allow singular human being to drop from our thoughts, we are fortunate that so many of the changes in patterns of extension and assemblage that this argument depends upon are already being realized with the erosion of standard adulthood and the proliferation of childhood ambiguities. The age of uncertainty, however, does not necessarily involve the improvement of children's lives. The multiplication of becoming may, in practice, take the form of the closure of schools, homelessness or states shirking their responsibilities toward children. Flexible adulthoods may turn out to place increasing emotional and financial burdens on children. We can see little improvement in children's living conditions in the majority world, and the benefits to children of fuller participation in consumer choice are far from certain. But we have seen some promising developments in the formation of assemblages that allow children to speak for themselves in the UN Convention and in changes in witnessing practices. In these new places for children, childhood ambiguities are managed through the patterning of extensions so that responsibility for them is shared by children, adults and adult institutions. In itself, the vocabulary of multiple becomings, assemblages and extensions is neither critical of nor supportive of the age of uncertainty. We offer it simply as an alternative to the two categories 'human being' and 'human becoming' that the age of uncertainty has problematized. Our new vocabulary is an alternative to terms that have become confused or confusing as the shape of people's lives has changed.

To broaden the vocabulary available to students of childhood, however, is also to alter the sensibilities and purposes of research. Rather than ask what prejudices currently limit children' powers and abilities, we can ask how adults 'become adult', what practical extensions are available to them that are denied to children. Where certain children seem to possess powers and abilities, we can ask what assemblages they are part of and whether membership of such assemblages may be extended to more children. But changing sensibilities and purposes of research is a complicated matter. As we add new ways of approaching questions of childhood, we do not want to lose any insights that have already been gained. So in the next chapter we will focus on how ideas of extension and multiple becoming can supplement and refine existing concerns of the social study of childhood.

8

Towards an immature sociology

Throughout this book, as we discussed the contributions of various students of childhood over the years, we have implied relationships between the times in which they wrote and the ideas that they built. We portrayed Parsons (1956) and Piaget (1955) as products of their time, suggesting that they took the assumptions of the developmental state as the basis of their sociological and psychological inquiries into the nature of childhood. We argued that present-day sociology of childhood, built throughout the 1990s, has turned against the assumptions of the developmental state in an attempt to recognize children as beings alongside adults. We have also noted that our own focus on childhood ambiguity, human incompleteness and extension is both a response to and a reflection of the flexible adulthoods and ambiguous childhoods of the age of uncertainty. To build an argument by drawing links between authors and their times is to rely on the assumption that no one writes or speaks outside of a context. Ideas are always closely related to their time and location. This is the basis of the claim we have consistently made that the being/becoming distinction, even though it is still an important aspect of the *regulation* of childhoods, is becoming 'outdated' as a way of *understanding* childhoods.

This chapter describes how our multiplication of becoming may influence the way that social research into childhood is conducted, how a change in sensitizing concepts may alter the pattern of questions that childhood researchers pose. The change we are urging on the social study of childhood is to pay less attention to the question of what children are in themselves, the question of being and becoming, and to pay more attention to the question of what children may become in changing contexts of extension and supplementation. But as we noted in Chapter 7, bringing about a change of this kind is difficult. It is one thing to advance a new set of slogans and quite another to change the pattern of what questions make sense to and seem important to people. To begin to do this one must link one's new sensitizing concepts with concerns that are already in place, and try to demonstrate how those new concepts address existing concerns more closely than before. So we have chosen to examine three key concerns of social research – agency, convention and ethics – in the light of incompleteness and multiple becoming. By the end of the chapter, then, we should have established both how the thought of incompleteness can inform social research into childhood and how this might be for the better. But first we need to understand how our three key concerns of social research currently shape the agenda of childhood studies.

Adulthood, confidence and truth regimes

Social research is never just about concepts and facts. It is also about feelings, especially feelings of confidence. One can often try to gain confidence in oneself and in one's actions by trying to live up to a socially recognized standard. The more standard one can appear, the less questionable one is and the more confident one can be. The majority of social researchers working today grew up in a world that still believed in standard adulthood and in human being as stable self-possession. Even though personal experiences may have led us to doubt the reality of standard adulthood in our own adult lives, the power of such standards lies in their ability to make us discount our personal experiences. If one experiences dependency, instability or lack of self-possession in adulthood, one can understand this as a fault in oneself rather than see existing standards as faulty. It can take enormous effort to reach a position whereby one judges social standards by one's experience rather than one's experience by social standards. The feminism we have touched on throughout the book represents just such an effort. Standard, Fordist adulthood, as we saw in Chapter 1, suited men's living conditions better than it suited women's. Mid-twentieth-century feminism, then, can be understood as an attempt to question that peculiar male bias in the industrial, western picture of a standard adult person, allowing women to gain confidence from their experiences against the backdrop of standards built to exclude them. The relationship between standard adulthood and confidence runs not only through people's more personal experiences but also through their working lives.

We noted in Chapter 3 that part of the appeal of the dominant framework lay in its ability to provide a ready answer to controversies around children and childhood. We saw how rapidly it could override and dispense with alternative visions of childhood, given by historians, by campaigners for children's rights or by children themselves. As a 'truth regime' the dominant framework provided a set of clear concepts through which to understand children, a set of facts concerning what children are like, and a set of feelings of confidence for adults. It informed adults that they, unlike children, were rational and fully aware of their culture's conventions. So, while the dominant framework informed adults of their duty to control children's lives, it also gave them the confidence in themselves, in their judgement and in their motivations to exert this control in practice.

As a truth regime then, the dominant framework helped adults to perform with certainty in situations that were in themselves uncertain, ambiguous or controversial. This confident certainty was achieved by clearly dividing the world into human beings and human becomings and, then, by distributing rights, duties and powers on this basis. So standard adulthood has been adults' most useful supplement when it comes to dealing with children. The truth regime had effects on adults as well as on children. If one's speech or actions were not in tune with the dominant framework, if one, for example, determined to base one's decisions more closely on what children had to say for themselves, then one could face the charge that one was not living up to standard adulthood, that one was forgetting one's responsibility to take responsibility for children. So to depart from the dominant framework, to recognize children as beings, or to refuse the being/becoming distinction is to open oneself to external criticism. But it is also to deprive oneself of the convenient fictions of adulthood that could otherwise make one feel confident in one's judgements and motivations.

By trying to recognize children as beings, our sociologies of childhood have challenged the dominant framework. By making this challenge they have deprived themselves of the easy confidence that comes when one is closely aligned with a standard. This position has been adopted for very good reasons. Too much confidence in their own powers and self-possession can lead adults unjustly to ignore children's voices, opinions and desires. But this left sociologists of childhood with a problem. Having abandoned one easy source of confidence, how could they then remain confident in their own research and arguments and ensure that others were confident in them as providers of valuable insights into children and childhood? How could they work against existing ideas and yet continue to make sense to and have influence on others as adults and as experts of good standing?

At one level, the path to confidence taken by sociologists of childhood resembles that taken by mid-twentieth-century feminism. This strategy reverses the normal relationship between socially recognized standards and experience, so that experience is deemed more trustworthy than standards, forms a basis for the rejection of those standards, and thereby becomes a source of confidence. For sociologists of childhood, 'experience' means the data that they produce about children through their research practice, data that can be used to expose the standard becoming view of childhood as inadequate or inaccurate. In order to counter socially prevalent views of children as becomings, then, they had to rely on another set of standards, those that specified what counts as good social research. Sociologists of childhood had the ability to remain confident even as they were challenging one supplementary source of confidence because they had access to another – the discipline of sociology. If they had not had access to this alternative supplement, the sociological standards that had been argued over, tested and, to some extent settled, over decades of sociological debate, it is difficult to see how they could have maintained confidence in themselves, let alone hope to persuade others of their case. This is a commendation, then, of the discipline of sociology as resource for those trying to bring about social change. But the sociological tradition, so necessary to the recognition of children as beings, itself arose and became settled in the same period of time that standard adulthood became 'standard'. Because of this, the sociological tradition has its own indebtedness to notions of completion, it has its own 'truth regime' that contains a commitment to being. In this sense we can speak of a 'mature' sociology. Perhaps the best way to illustrate this claim is to spend a little time describing mature sociology as a 'problem space'.

Mature sociology as a problem space

One of the most striking features of societies is that they involve a high degree of coordination between the activities of the different individual people and groups that they are composed of. Even though different individuals and different groups may have different desires, opinions and motivations from each other, societies themselves seem to be (more or less) orderly and consistent. Over the years, sociologists have tried to discover and to describe the reasons behind the existence of social order. They have tried to figure out how the potential for disorder that the differences between individuals and groups presents can ever be held in check. So the problem of social order is one element of the problem space of the discipline of sociology. This problem has received many different answers, but one answer has been particularly popular. If people differ and societies thus have the potential to become disorderly, then there must be something in society that is capable of preventing disorder. This 'something' has gone by many names. Durkheim (1964) described it as the 'collective conscience', a set of ideas and values held in common by the majority of society's members regardless of their circumstances. Marx and Engels (1970) described it as 'ideology', a picture of society held by the majority of society's members that convinces them that society is just and fair. Parsons (1951) gave his own names to this 'something' – values, roles and expectations. Though each of these social thinkers tells quite a different story about societies, Marx (Marx and Engels 1999) deploring the injustices of capitalism, Durkheim (1964) warning us of the dangers of the erosion of collective conscience, each tries to explain social order by referring to *convention*. Though people differ one from another, as long as they hold certain mutual expectations, values or beliefs in common, disorder can be held in check. Convention is understood to have the power to knit all the different elements of society into one more or less consistent whole. Society is always ready to unravel itself, but is constantly being converted from a disparate disunity to an orderly unity. Convention, then, is given the role of completing society, filling the gaps that exist between different individuals and groups.

Another feature of societies that has been just as apparent to sociologists, however, is 'change'. Change is our second element of the problem space of the discipline of sociology. Even though societies are more or less orderly, they can also change over time and sociologists throughout the years have tried to give account of this. If convention has the function of completing social order, then for that order to change there must be something in society that is to some extent independent of convention. If we briefly examine the work of some very influential social thinkers we shall find out what that 'something' is. Marx and Engels (1999) wanted capitalist society to change through a communist revolution. In an attempt to bring revolution about, they worked to build knowledge of society that gave an alternative to conventional ideology, knowledge that would galvanize and consolidate a consciousness among the industrial working class that society could and should change radically. They wanted to change working people's interpretation of society so as to turn them into *agents* of change who could choose to build communism and could act on that choice. Weber's (1964) approach to the problem of change was rather different, but shared an emphasis on interpretation and choice. He tried to explain why capitalism, with its close links to the use of technology in the manufacture of goods, arose in western Europe rather than in other parts of the world, such as China, that were just as technologically advanced as early modern Europe, if not more so. He argued that capitalism emerged in Europe because early European industrialists chose to adopt religious principles, which he calls the Protestant Ethic. These principles led them to save their profits for reinvestment in business, to use them as capital rather than to spend them on luxurious ostentation. For both Marx and Engels (1999) and Weber (1964), social change is possible because people have the power to interpret their lives outside of existing convention and so to act against existing convention. Where convention tends to hold society in stasis, people's independent *agency* can bring about change.

So far, then, we have seen that mature sociology has generated two figures – 'convention' and 'agency' – each of which stands as an answer to one or other element of sociology's problem space. Both of these answers are consistent, however, with features of standard adulthood. Convention addresses anxieties about social disorder. It assuages those anxieties by promising completeness and consistency. In the face of the facts of social change, the figure of agency was developed to provide something that was independent of convention and was thus able to work against it. Completeness and independence have been touchstones of sociological thought for many years, completeness lodged within the model of convention, independence lodged within the model of agency. To use mature sociology as a supplementary source of confidence, one must be able to speak its language, but speaking its language can commit one to ways of thinking that are indebted to standard adulthood.

There is a third element in sociology's problem space – ethics. If one is concerned with society's stability and change, one is also concerned with the relative well-being of the people and groups who constitute society. If one examines existing social arrangements to find inequality or injustice one may desire social change. On the other hand one may find some features of social arrangements that one would wish to preserve. Sociology's problem of ethics is to decide which features to try to change and which to try to preserve. Often, then, as a sociologist one is faced with a decision; is one to use one's independent agency to support the conventions that currently complete society, or is one to use it to develop alternative ways of completing society, alternative visions of desirable social order? If one is to play any part as a sociologist in shaping society, it seems, one must begin with a clear ethical position, for or against one convention or another. If one allows one's position to change over time, it seems, this will diminish one's chances of making any impact on society at all. Just as sociology's problem space can lead us to think in terms of completion and independence, so it also calls for *stable* ethical positions. As a supplementary source of confidence, mature sociology would seem to ask those who rely on it to think in terms of, and to value, completion, independence and stability. We shall now argue that sociologies of childhood, relying on mature sociology as a source of confidence and credibility, have listened to this request and responded to it.

Maturing the sociology of childhood

We believe . . . that it would be a mistake to think that the theorising of childhood should, or can, take place outside of the theoretical debates of mainstream sociology . . . That outcome would relieve other branches of sociology from the necessity of thinking through the implications for their own treatment of childhood.

(James and Prout 1997: 24)

As the quotation above indicates, sociologists of childhood are well aware of their dependence on mature sociology for their confidence and credibility. It is clear that in order to enjoy sociology as a supplement they must accept the problem space of mainstream sociology and continue to discuss childhood through the notions of convention, agency and ethics as we have described them above. It is only by sharing a vocabulary and problem space with the older, more mature tradition of mainstream sociology that the younger, less developed subdiscipline of the sociology of childhood can hope to win confidence and have influence. For sociologists of childhood to use convention, agency and ethics in the ways established within the parent discipline is for them to make their work 'mature'. If the sociology of childhood made no attempt to mature itself, then like the children it studies, it would be in danger of not being recognized. As we shall now see, this desire for maturity has had significant effects on the debates and approaches that sociologists of childhood have developed.

In Chapter 3 we surveyed three different approaches to the social study of childhood. We noted that there were some important differences between these approaches, but that despite these differences they shared an opposition to the conventional view of children as becomings and an ethic that committed them to recognizing children as beings. Recognizing children as beings meant recognizing them in sociological terms as 'agents'. In ethnography, children were recognized as agents alongside adults since they were deemed capable of forming their own interpretations and views of other people and of their social interaction. In the standpoint approach children were recognized as a group of agents whose interpretations and views of the social world were systematically suppressed by power differences between adults and children. In the macro-analytic approach the suppression of children's agency was understood to take the form of the failure to use generation as a sociological variable. In each case, to recognize children as beings is to argue that an existing convention or way of completing social order should be replaced with a new convention – the view that children, like adults, are social agents capable of independent interpretation and action. In this context any portrayal of children as becomings is, ethically speaking, a retrograde step.

The appeal of the dominant framework lay in its ability to bring clarity and order to situations that were controversial or contradictory. As a convention it provided a single view of children that could suppress varied and contradictory views of children to bring orderly completion. In their opposition to the dominant framework sociologies of childhood have developed a similar, singular view of childhood as a state of being because they have been supported by the standard concepts of their parent discipline. Children have been recategorized as beings and as active social agents, but this recategorization has depended on a view of social life that is clearly compatible with the standards of standard adulthood – completion, independence and stability. Children, it seems, can be recategorized as beings as long as we accept that conventions are capable of completing social order, that agency is something held in independence and that an ethical approach to the study of social life will be based on a stable position. As the sociology of childhood 'matures' itself, then, it accepts a picture of the social world and of the role of the sociologist within society that is peculiarly dependent on being.

Sociological maturity as a compromise

It has, arguably, been necessary for the sociology of childhood to mature itself in the way we have described. After all, standard mainstream sociological thought has been helpful in providing sociologists of childhood with an alternative source of confidence in their work. It has helped them to remain credible even as they have argued against a view of children as 'becomings' that still has wide currency. To use the discipline of sociology as a supplement requires that one accept a certain problem space and the concepts that go with it. But in the light of the studies presented in Part two, this 'maturity' would appear to have some costs. The more certain one is that children belong in the category 'being', the less likely one is to notice either the erosion of the category, or that being and becoming can overlap in children's lives to produce childhood ambiguity. The more one takes the view that convention completes social order, the less one will be sensitive to the subtle changes in the function of family homes and schools that are retaining a view of children as incomplete while also allowing them a degree of independent thought and action. The more committed one is to an ethic that recognizes children as beings, the less sensitive one will be to the recognition of children that comes with their status as dependent becomings, such as we have seen in the UN Convention on the Rights of the Child. As standard adulthood is eroded and as childhood ambiguities multiply, the sociology of childhood's reliance on completeness, independence and stability looks increasingly like a compromise between sociological confidence and the ability to grasp the significance of the age of uncertainty for childhood.

These arguments raise some simple but important questions. Should the sociology of childhood continue to think of itself as in need of 'permission' from its parent discipline? Should it try to live up to those mainstream, mature sociological standards that are so closely related to standard adulthood? Should it strive for confidence by trying to establish a new, single conventional view of childhood that is driven by a stable ethical position? If mature sociological standards were the only available source of confidence the answer to all of these questions would be 'yes'. But, as we have seen in Chapter 7, different ways of thinking that allow for incompleteness and multiple becoming are available to us. If the sociology of childhood supplemented itself through these ideas, it might not only change itself, but also help to change its parent discipline. The risk involved in this is that the sociology of childhood will become 'immature' and lose recognition, but the benefit is that it might open itself and its parent discipline to new ways of thinking about society that are compatible with the conditions of the age of uncertainty.

Elements of an immature sociology

The philosophers we examined in Chapter 7 were working toward the end of the period of Fordist stability. Their work emerged in a context that was critical of ideas of 'completeness' especially the promise of complete control that, on their view, lay within Fordist coordination of government, industry and population. On our reading, Derrida (1976) called complete, independent and stable standard adulthood into question by exposing the limits of 'self-presence', while Deleuze and Guattari (1988) sought to draw our attention to the incompleteness, dependency, variety and flux of human life by examining it through the notion of 'assemblage'. These ideas are stimulating and, coming as they do at the beginnings of the age of uncertainty, have a certain openness to flexibility and ambiguity. However, they can hardly be said to add up to a sociology.

If we are to develop an 'immature sociology' (Lee 1998c) that is both open to the flexibilities and ambiguities of the age of uncertainty and confident enough to inform its parent discipline, we cannot expect philosophy to provide all the answers. Fortunately, the discipline of sociology contains approaches that have not aligned themselves with standard adulthood. It contains its own immaturities. While these approaches are not mainstream, they may nevertheless prove useful to us in assembling an immature sociology. So in the following sections we shall give a brief survey of these approaches, drawing them together through the themes of dependency, incompleteness and instability.

Agency as dependency

As we have seen, sociology often uses 'agency' to account for social change. Agents are understood to be able to act against convention to bring change, because they are in some way 'independent' of convention. There would seem to be a part of each social agent that is able to form interpretations of the social world that differ from convention. It is their independent possession of the faculty of interpretation that allows agents to act in unconventional ways. This picture of the agent bears a strong resemblance to the independent figure of the self-present person that Derrida (1976) drew our attention to. It is the agent's self-possession that allows the agent to differ from convention in his or her interpretations. If our social surroundings are ordered, completed and secured by convention it would seem that there must be some part of each agent that owes nothing to those social surroundings.

There is much to commend this picture of agency. It not only finds a place in sociology's problem space, but also lends a good deal of encouragement to any who would wish to change their circumstances. If one considers oneself an agent, one can always have faith in one's self-possessed independence, whatever the social circumstances. But where does the self-possession of the agent come from? This is the basic question posed by a sociological approach to agency that is often referred to as actor network theory (ANT) (Latour 1987, 1988; Law 1998). The answer that ANT has developed is rather interesting. ANT suggests that the more a person appears to possess agency and the more independently self-present they appear, the more dependent that person is for their powers and identity as an agent on a network of extensions (Lee 1998b).

Perhaps the clearest example of the ANT approach to agency can be found in Latour's (1988) treatment of Louis Pasteur, the inventor of 'pasteurization', a process for preventing the growth of harmful bacteria in cow's milk. Pasteur is often thought of as a genius, a singularly independent thinker. It seems that he single-handedly changed conventional ways of dealing with milk, making it safer to drink and bringing about a wide-spread improvement in health. Pasteur, then, was an agent of change. But Latour (1988) asks where Pasteur's 'agency' came from. Did Pasteur separate himself in some way from the conventional order that surrounded him, and then return to the world with his 'pasteurization' fully formed? On Latour's (1988) account such a picture is far from the truth. In developing the process of pasteurization, Pasteur had to build a network of other 'actors' that he could depend upon. Some of these 'actors' were material in nature; for example, in order to process milk he had to develop specialized equipment that he could depend upon. Some of these 'actors' were political; for example, in order to have others adopt pasteurization he needed allies who thought that untreated milk was a significant threat to health. Other 'actors' were simply his collaborators and employees. The process of building this mutually dependent network of equipment, people and political alliances was the building of pasteurization, and Pasteur was just one element of it. As an agent he was never independently outside his social world. Instead he was deeply involved in it and thoroughly dependent on certain elements of it for his agency. Over the years, this network has grown in scale and scope to include government policy-makers, the combined dairy farms of whole countries and huge populations of milk consumers. As pasteurization spread, more and more actors extended the network and became invested in it. As the network has grown, so has Pasteur's reputation as an independent actor.

ANT gives an account of agency that does not rely on the independence and self-possession of the standard adult. Instead it emphasizes incompleteness and dependency. Without his network of extensions and supplements, for example, Pasteur would not have been the agent for change we see him as today. But we have grown used to thinking of agency as independence because it is so easy to forget dependencies, extensions and supplements. Simply stated, the story of Pasteur as independent genius is easier to tell than the story of all his dependencies.

To illustrate the relevance of the ANT approach to childhood, we can briefly return to the example of child witnesses in the criminal courts of England and Wales. As we argued in Chapter 6, children's performance as independent witnesses has been assisted by the addition of extensions. The child witness becomes more agentic and can pass as more self-present as more 'actors' are added to their 'network'. Video-cameras, videotape, television screens, and the police and social workers who help children to produce their testimony all contribute to redistributing the burden of childhood ambiguity so that it does not all come to rest on child witnesses' shoulders. Actor networks are very much like Deleuze and Guattari's (1988) 'assemblages'. The assemblage/actor network approach to agency does not assume that agency is or can be 'possessed' by people in independence of their surroundings. The principal advantage of this approach is that, since it does not assume that agency is a simple possession, it opens agency up to empirical study and analysis. We can ask what a given person, whether adult or child, depends upon for their agency. So with this approach to agency, instead of asking whether children, like adults, possess agency or not, we can ask how agency is built or may be built for them by examining the extensions and supplements that are available to them.

Incomplete conventions

If agency can be understood through dependency, can convention be understood as incomplete? Could convention be understood as an open-ended *process* of making sense and producing order rather than as a stable set of shared values or principles? In the view outlined above, convention seemed to sit outside the turmoil and contradiction of social life. It had its own coherence and consistency that gave it the ability to lead societies into order against their tendency toward disorder. On this view, it would seem that social life is *governed* by convention, and is lived after conventions are known. But what if convention did not have this power to govern? What if social life were conducted in search of convention and in search of order rather than on the basis of conventions that are already known? This is the view advanced by the sociological tradition of ethnomethodology (Garfinkel 1967; Turner 1974; Heritage 1984; Livingstone 1987). For ethnomethodologists, people never have access to a full set of rules to govern their conduct. People do not live *out of* conventions, but instead, live *in search* of conventions. For ethnomethodologists, participation in social life is not simply a matter of 'knowing one's place', but is rather a matter of facing up to the question 'how are we to proceed?' If there is 'social order' then this is the result of temporary and local settlements among social participants of what conventions they should apply to themselves and to each other. These settlements are reached through negotiation. This does not mean to say that people never refer to 'convention' in their negotiations. Indeed, one way to settle such a negotiation is precisely to refer to a convention or commonly held view and to invite others to treat this as a rule. Ethnomethodologists point out, however, that there is never any guarantee that others will accept such a suggested convention and agree to live by the rule it offers.

So we now have two different views of convention. On one view convention is complete and completing, governing people's conduct by informing them of rules, values and norms. On the other, convention is an ongoing process of the creation of rules, values and norms that are local and temporary in their effects. The view of convention as an 'endless, ongoing' accomplishment (Garfinkel 1967: 1) differs markedly from that offered by Parsons (1956). In Chapter 3 we noted that for Parsons (1956) stable values and norms come before each person in society. Socialization is a process of learning those stable conventions so as to become a complete human being. From the ethnomethodological point of view, we cannot presume that there are stable conventions to learn. So just as ANT opened agency to empirical examination and analysis, so ethnomethodology opens convention to empirical examination and analysis. Rather than being presumed to exist, if convention seems to be at work, it must be accounted for in terms of people's negotiations.

From our perspective, the ethnomethodological view has the distinct advantage of allowing us to find out about convention without committing ourselves to completion. But it also has its limitations. Because it is so concerned with people's negotiation of temporary and local answers to the question 'how are we to proceed?' it often seems to forget that these negotiations take place in a wider context and that this wider context has a history. This issue comes to a head when we consider the dominant framework as a source of conventions about how to treat children. It seems to be the case that it has been easy for adults to decide how they are to proceed when dealing with children by referring to the dominant framework. The dominant framework provides a convention whereby children are dependent and so should be protected, guided or socialized but not necessarily recognized as having views and opinions of their own. The dominant framework, then, provides adults with a resource for creating social order, a resource that may be deployed or ignored depending on the outcome of local negotiation. But ethnomethodology does not answer the question of where this resource itself came from and how it came to be so widely available. How did the conventions of the dominant framework become stable enough to last over time and across different contexts? If an immature sociology is to give sociologists of childhood the confidence to address the conditions of the age of uncertainty, and if it is to build on ethnomethodological insights, it will need to face up to this problem.

We have already touched on this problem in Chapter 2, when we asked how childhood came to be so widely associated with dependency. If we briefly redescribe the answer we offered it should become clear that the ethnomethodological view of convention as process and the actor network/assemblage view of the importance of extension, if used together, can produce a reasonable answer. We found the origins of the association between childhood and dependency in the 'preservation' of children. The preservation of children was not just a set of ideas. It was also a set of practices in which children came to be surrounded by extensions that separated them from mainstream social life. Parents, teachers and the walls of the family home and the classroom were all 'added' on to children, extending them into their own futures and into the future of the state while at the same time protecting them from 'undesirable' influences. Children under preservation became part of a network that linked them to reasons of state and channelled their agency into their development, socialization and education. The conventional view of children as dependent that emerged was part of this actor network or assemblage. The conventional view of children as dependent was stable enough to carry over time and across places because it was built into the preservation network of the developmental state. It prospered as a convention as the preservation network grew to include more people, more buildings, more regulations and, by the mid-twentieth century, the knowledges of childhood provided by Parsons (1956) and Piaget (1955).

Conventions, then, do not govern society from the 'outside' but emerge alongside and receive strength from assemblages that they are consistent with. They do not create social order, but are part of social orders that are created. As an assemblage grows, so its accompanying conventions come to seem more and more reliable. They take on the appearance of truth. Truth regimes, then are built of materials and practices as well as ideas. But since assemblages are open-ended, they are never complete. Thus even though conventions are stable enough to be applied over time and across different places they are always open to change and replacement, on the condition that materials and persons are assembled in ways that are consistent with their change or replacement.

Ethics in motion

In Chapter 3 we saw that various sociologies of childhood found an ethical basis in the claim that since children are beings they deserve recognition. Particular attention was given to listening to children's voices in order to hear and take account of their views, opinions and desires. There is nothing objectionable in this. It is a timely recognition of the extent to which the mediation of children by adults has served not only to protect children, but also to silence them. As such the ethical recognition of children as beings is a sound guide to adult social researcher's conduct toward children.

As we have argued above, mature sociology requires those who seek confidence in it to adopt stable ethical positions. The need to hold on to such stable ethical positions, however, causes certain difficulties in the application of the sociology of childhood's ethic of recognition. Since mediation by adults has often silenced children, it would seem to be desirable for any sociologist of childhood to seek children's unmediated voices and to pass those unmediated voices on to a wider audience. Thus James and Prout (1997: 8) write: 'Ethnography is a particularly useful method for the study of childhood. It offers children a more direct voice and participation in the production of sociological data.' The implication is that the closer a methodology takes us to the goal of children's unmediated speech, the more ethically adequate that methodology will be.

Despite seeking ethical adequacy in children's unmediated speech, James and Prout (1997: 8) acknowledge that ethnography allows only a '*more* direct voice' for children. In a similar vein, although James (1996: 315) advances a claim to write from the child's perspective, she does not 'make claims to reveal the authentic child but, more humbly, to provide a rendering of what childhood might be like'.

Mature sociology's requirement of ethical stability and consistency then can lead sociologists of childhood on a quest for the unmediated self-presence of the child. It generates an anxiety that by listening to children and by acting as their messengers sociologists of childhood themselves may unwittingly do children an injustice by mediating them.

If we accept Derrida's (1976) arguments about the limits of self-presence, however, we would find that children's unmediated self-presence is not available to us. All that is possible is to mediate children well. The ethical consistency and stability called for by mature sociology then is thrown into confusion. Rather than being supported by a firm ethical decision to recognize children as beings, this very act of recognition opens up a fresh series of questions such as what is to count as 'good' mediation. If all we can do is mediate and if we cannot bring our ethical work to a close by discovering the 'authentic' child, then we need to think of ethics outside the terms of stable positions. At one level, to choose to recognize children as beings rather as becomings may be preferable. But this choice does not lead us to a stable position of ethical adequacy. So rather than think of ethics as a set of stable positions we might instead think of ethics as 'motion'. Rather than ask whether one ethical stance is better than another, we can instead ask whether particular patterns of the extension or mediation of children open movements and transfers of voice that are desirable. What are the benefits of taking such a view of the sociology of childhood as an ethical enterprise?

On the 'being' view of childhood, any portrayal of children as becomings is a retrograde step. Thus if we wanted our ethical position to be stable enough to give us confidence, we would find the emphasis that some sections of the UN Convention on the Rights of the Child give to children's status as human becomings objectionable. Considered through an ethics of motion, however, we can see that this use of the becoming view of childhood can form the basis of possible transfers of children's views through networks of mediation that bypass states, state representatives and even parents. A desirable opportunity for children may emerge then from a quite unexpected place. While it may suit social researchers to assure themselves that children are beings, it may not always suit children. While an ethics of motion cannot provide social researchers with the confidence that they will always know their position, it can nevertheless still provide opportunities to make judgements. It opens the process of making such judgements to the possibility of unexpected change, and, by keeping the work of making judgements open in this way it also allows space to take account of children's own preferences.

Conclusion

In this chapter we presented the sociology of childhood and, by implication, mature sociology in general, with a problem. The problem was how to adapt to the conditions of the age of uncertainty, with its erosion of being and production of ambiguities, without losing confidence. This chapter certainly cannot pretend to have provided all the answers. Nevertheless it has shown that the resources are available for the sociology of childhood to become immature without abandoning the problem space of its parent discipline. Even though an immature sociology would not accept views of agency as independence, of convention as completion or of ethics as a set of stable positions it is still able to address questions of social order, of social change and of the rights and wrongs of order and change.

Having given some indication of how the sociology of childhood may respond to the age of uncertainty, in the next chapter we can begin to draw some conclusions. As well as offering a brief survey of the argument presented throughout the book, we shall also turn to a question that we have not so far explicitly stated: in the absence of a clear division between human beings and human becomings, what are we to make of 'growing up'?

9

Conclusion: growing up and slowing down

Over the course of this book we have given examples of children's 'places' in society. We have seen how those places are changing as societies are changing in what we have called the age of uncertainty. Sometimes changes in children's places are being deliberately engineered (see Chapter 6). Sometimes they are coming about as a by-product of broader developments (see Chapters 4 and 5). Whether these changes are deliberate or accidental, however, they take the form of alterations in the patterns of extension, the networks or assemblages, that children (and adults) find themselves involved in. Along the way, we have outlined the reasons why there is a field of inquiry called the 'sociology of childhood' and we have examined some of the key approaches that constitute that field. We have also offered a range of new sensitizing concepts to help the sociology of childhood to respond to the social conditions of the age of uncertainty.

For all this, however, we seem to have said very little about growing up. There are some very good reasons for avoiding this topic entirely. It is still hard to think of children changing over time without accepting the terms of the dominant framework. This is because it seems hard to chart and to describe change unless one has a fixed finishing point, such as journey's end or standard, complete adulthood, to refer to. Further, any general description of what growing up is like would risk creating yet another universal figure of *the* child that might obscure differences between children as individual persons or between the different 'childhoods' that are constituted by wider socio-economic and cultural variation. This may be why sociologies of childhood have not, thus far, developed an alternative view of growing up to rival that offered by the dominant framework. As we argued in Chapter 8, however, unless such an alternative is offered, the sociology of childhood will be unable to communicate to a wider audience on an issue that, for many, is still the central question of childhood.

In this chapter we shall attempt to outline a picture of growing up that is quite different from the picture offered by the dominant framework. Using some of our new sensitizing concepts, and taking heed of human incompleteness, we shall try to link the dominant framework's concern for social and personal order with the sociology of childhood's even-handed approach to adults and children. One way of thinking about the difference between the dominant framework and the sociology of childhood is in terms of their approaches to 'time'. When it deploys and reinforces the being/becoming distinction, the dominant framework tends to treat chronological age as the variable that distinguishes between its two types of humans. Time, understood as chronological age, is the backbone along which the dominant framework arranges all the other forms of human variation that it recognizes, such as rational-irrational, cultural-natural and competent-incompetent (Hutchby and Moran-Ellis 1998). Since the sociology of childhood refuses to distinguish between two types of humans, it tends to deal with the here and now of children's voices and agency. Its picture of human variation tends to dispense with the backbone of chronological age. The macro-analytic approach (see Chapter 3) is something of an exception to this. It promises to chart medium and long-term change in childhood as a social category. But such a historical treatment of time does not have the personal and experiential resonances of growing up.

As we build our alternative picture of growing up, we shall accept that time is an important source of human variation, but we shall also try to show that it is just *one* source of such variation, taking its place alongside variations in the assemblages that humans, whether children or adults, involve themselves in. In our alternative picture of growing up, time is not a single straight spine along which people travel and against which their progress can be measured. Instead, time is like a river with many eddies, whirlpools, patches of white water and currents, all running and changing at different speeds (Serres 1982). On this view, growing up is what happens as networks or assemblages of extension expand and incorporate more and more elements. The bigger the assemblage, the slower it can change or be changed. From this perspective, growing up is a *slowing down*, a decrease in the rate at which a person can pass from one social order to another. Slowing down or growing up has a cost. It sets limits to the pace of personal and social change. But it also has a benefit. The more extensive one's network, the more elements included in one's assemblage, the more powerfully agentic one can be. For the moment, this picture of growing up is rather abstract. Later on we shall illustrate it further with some concrete examples. But before we turn to our new picture of growing up, let's take the opportunity to review some of the key arguments we have presented so far.

Summary and review

We began the book with a question. Why is there a UN Declaration of Human Rights *and* a UN Convention on the Rights of the Child? Why, in other words, does it seem to have been accepted at the level of global regulation that there are two types of humans? Chapters 1 and 2 were an attempt to answer this question. The adult/child division in global regulation is a reflection of a widely held view that adults are human beings while children are human becomings (Qvortrup 1994). But what factors made this distinction seem so important and so credible?

Chapter 1 tried to account for the understanding of adults as beings. We argued that the image of the standard adult was, for a time, so well supported by the socio-economic conditions of Fordism (Harvey 1989) that a view of adults as stable, complete, self-possessed beings seemed to be true. Chapter 2 tried to account for the general understanding of children as becomings and the particular understanding of children as dependent becomings. We argued that these understandings of children arose as the leaders of western European states began to think about their states' future economic and political position relative to their trading and military rivals. As states began to colonize their own futures, children became identified as sites of investment. Appropriate investment in children promised a successful future for the state. This led to efforts to preserve children that, in turn, separated children from mainstream society and made their lives and opportunities dependent on the decisions of parents and childcare experts. Within the developmental state, children were both separated from the here and now of social life and given more or less clearly demarcated destinies. This established the becoming view of childhood. So the images of standard adulthood and of dependent childhood, both supported by the socio-economic and political relations that held within states, came together in the twentieth century to provide a binary view of human variation which allowed for two types of humans – beings and becomings – each with their own different characteristics.

Chapters 1 and 2 also told the story of how the certainties and assumptions about adults and children that held good under Fordism and under the developmental state came to be challenged in the late twentieth century. As trade became increasingly globalized, the close relations of mutual interdependence between states, businesses and populations that had been established under Fordism could no longer be maintained. As part of a general tendency away from Fordism and toward 'flexible accumulation' (Harvey 1989), adult working lives were opened to greater flexibility and uncertainty. Under these conditions, adulthood could no longer be understood as journey's end because adults now had to be able to change. Adults' intimate lives were also opened to flexibility and uncertainty as the relationship between male gender and breadwinner status was undermined. This opened the way for feminism to challenge traditional family roles and for stable romantic love to be replaced by provisional 'confluent relationships' (Giddens 1992). In this age of uncertainty, even adults began to find it hard to reach the standards of standard adulthood.

As to the developmental state and its treatment of children as dependent becomings, the globalization of trade and the development of global regulation of childhood has begun to erode the sense in which states *own* their populations as a resource. While investment in children has continued into the age of uncertainty, children's status as becomings now qualifies them for a kind of independence from reasons of state. The relationship between states and their children is no longer a simple relationship between investor and sites of investment. It has become ambiguous in the sense that children are both dependent and independent in their status as becomings. Chapters 1 and 2 gave us good reasons to believe that while the being/becoming division is still significant for the *regulation* of relationships between adults and children, the assumptions it involves no longer provide us with a sound basis for attempts to *understand or describe* contemporary childhoods.

Chapter 3 compared two ways of understanding childhood – the dominant framework and the sociology of childhood. We saw how closely the dominant framework based itself on the being/becoming division and how various sociologies of childhood rejected that division on, primarily, ethical and political grounds. The dominant framework, it seemed, had helped to silence children over the years. Sociologies of childhood can be seen as a response to the age of uncertainty, as an attempt to consolidate the opportunities for the recognition of children that the breakdown of standard adulthood presents. But, as we saw, its main strategy involved emptying the 'becoming' category and putting children alongside adults in the 'being' category. The problem with this was that our picture of being, with all its stability and completion, no longer seems credible. We then raised the question of how we are to go about studying childhoods when neither 'being' nor 'becoming' can be presented as adequate models of childhood.

In Part two, we surveyed some of the places of children in society. We saw that the growing numbers of children out of place across the world were the result of the responses of governmental and international policy-makers' responses to the age of uncertainty. The structural adjustment programmes devised to make the economies of the South more flexible had increased rates of child poverty and homelessness, while decreasing states' ability to invest in their children. The result was a mismatch between the model of the developmental state and the financial resources of southern states. This produced categories of ambiguous children, who could be understood neither as beings nor as becomings. These children, we argued, often bear the burden of their state's problems. We saw that similar conditions apply to some of the poorer children of the North.

As we considered children 'in their place' we argued that late-twentieth-century technological and economic change means that childhood ambiguities are also arising in the very heart of the developmental state. The institutions of home and school are becoming increasingly penetrated by media that connect children to a wider world across the boundaries of 'preservation'. Due primarily to television, children in the family home are both dependent becomings and relatively independent actors in the economy because they are now in a position to make consumer choices from within their cocoon.

In Chapter 6, we saw how some contemporary bids to regulate childhood are facing up to childhood's ambiguity. Rather than attempt to resolve childhood ambiguities, the UN Convention on the Rights of the
Child had to accept and work with that ambiguity. As a set of promises,
it offers opportunities for the burden of childhood ambiguity to be distributed among states, adults and children rather than come to rest solely
on children's shoulders. When we examined the introduction of video-
technology to child-witnessing in the criminal courts of England and
Wales, we made a similar case. Here, the problem that childhood ambiguity
presented to courts was not resolved, but was rather redistributed to help
children pass as witnesses.

Throughout Part two we began to form the view that the nature of
childhood varies with the social and technological contexts that surround
children. In all the examples we studied, questions of whether children
really are beings or becomings seemed much less important to our understanding of children's places in society than questions about how children
were extended by other people and by their physical, financial and technological surroundings. We had already argued in Part one that the terms
of the being/becoming debate between the dominant framework and
sociologies of childhood had become less than helpful in the age of uncertainty. The bases of inquiry into the relationship between childhood and
society had become unclear. So in Chapter 7 we searched for different ways
of thinking about human life, ways that were not reliant on images of
adulthood as complete, stable, self-possessed being. We found a wealth of
such sensitizing concepts in the work of philosophers, who were themselves responding to the social and political conditions of Fordism just as
Fordism gave way to the age of uncertainty. These philosophers helped us
to see human life as a matter of continual change, dependency and becoming. With their help we emptied the category 'being' and multiplied 'becoming' beyond the boundaries that the developmental state and the
dominant framework had set around it. Even though the being/becoming
distinction between adults and children was as real as the patterns of extension that support it, it was only ever one kind of variation between human
becomings in a context of many others. Human becomings are as varied as
the range of assemblages that they are involved in and borrow their powers
from. Once we found the sensitizing concepts we needed to address the
ambiguities of the age of uncertainty, we began in Chapter 8 to relate these
concepts to sociological tradition. We tried to show how sociologists of
childhood could become confident enough to use these concepts in their
research.

Growing up: adulthood, childhood and speed

Now that we have reviewed the main features of the book so far, we can
turn to the difficult task of rethinking growing up for the age of uncer-

tainty and in the absence of journey's end. The approach to the social study of childhood offered in this book is based on a strategy of emptying 'being' and multiplying 'becoming'. At first glance it might seem to share a problem with existing 'being-based' sociologies of childhood. By putting all humans in the same category, it would seem to ignore the relationship between childhood and time that has been so successfully explored within the dominant framework. Having outlined the central commitments of our new approach, however, we are now in a position to outline a new account of that important relationship.

Traditionally, growing up has been seen as a movement from disorder to order. For Parsons (1956) knowledge of convention allows grown-ups to regulate their own conduct in a way that coordinates them with the conduct of other members of society. For Piaget (1955) growing up involves an accommodation of patterns of thought and reason to fit the order of the physical world. In both cases then grown-ups are taken to be intrinsically more orderly than children. Our alternative approach to growing up involves a rather different assumption about age and order. If children appear disorderly this is not because their activities simply lack order. Rather it is because their activities contain a profusion of different orders which they can move between very rapidly. A brief examination of children's play can provide us with an illustration of this.

In play, a plastic wrench need have nothing to do with games of home or car maintenance. When it is used as a prop or extension to realize a game of 'surgery' it can become a surgical instrument – it can help to establish an orderly relationship between surgeon and patient. The patient must lie still while the surgeon works on the patient's abdomen. But sudden changes to this orderly assemblage of persons, conventions and extensions can occur. Perhaps the patient is no longer in need of abdominal surgery. The plastic wrench can travel to the mouth and become a dental tool for the extraction of rotten teeth. The patient must now sit up and be ready to rinse the mouth with fluid from a toy teacup brought into play from an arm's length away. A new orderly assemblage has been produced that maintains a relationship of authority between patient and medical practitioner even as their roles change. This new assemblage involves some elements of the old order, such as the plastic wrench and the two human participants, but also incorporates some fresh elements, such as a different chair and the toy teacup. No matter how rapidly they may change, the orders we have described involve real materials, real people, real relationships and real conventions. These orders are real even though they are fleeting. To point out that the 'surgeon' is not properly qualified and is not therefore a real surgeon would be to miss the point. It would reflect a delirium of 'realism' rather than a fair assessment of what is being achieved.

If we have established the real but fleeting nature of orders produced in play, how does play differ from typical grown-up activities? If we think there is a difference it certainly cannot be based on the notion that play is merely pretend while grown-up activities are real. So let us explore an example of serious grown-up activity from the perspective of assemblages. Since criminal courts have often had difficulty with children precisely on the basis of children's 'disorderly' minds, we shall focus on courtroom activity. What makes courtroom activity more serious than children's play? For one thing criminal trials take place in specially designed rooms that assign physical positions to the various members of the court. Judge, jury, lawyers, witnesses, the accused and the general public each have their own special place. People are employed to make sure that those who are unfamiliar with courtroom settings find, and in the case of the accused, remain in their proper places. If the general public give strong vocal support to the accused and thereby seek to convert their proper place from one of silent observation to one of loud protest, the judge has legal sanctions at their disposal to threaten this reordering of the courtroom assemblage into quiescence.

Adults in courtrooms then have more extensions available to them than children at play typically have. These extensions help to slow down any change to the order of the court. Perhaps the greatest difference between the assemblages of play and those of criminal proceedings is that the courtroom assemblage is connected to a further assemblage of prison officers and places of detention. Once a verdict has been reached, it can form the basis of a stable order that can last for years – the incarceration of the accused in a building and among personnel whose express purpose is to maintain the order of guilt.

From this perspective, growing up is a matter of the slowing of the pace of change between orders. It is an increase in the range and number of extensions available to us. It is also an increase in the range and stability of our actions. The courtroom is in itself no more or less 'pretend' than the 'surgery' assemblage we described above. It simply involves more people and materials and, consequently, changes much more slowly. This general account of growing up does not imply that all experience of childhood is identical. Growing up is as diverse in its major and minor currents, its eddies and whirlpools as is the range of human extension.

Becoming to an end

Even though we chose to examine growing up by comparing a play sequence and courtroom activity, it is clear that children are not always at play and adults are not always involved in serious activities. Children experience plenty of slowing at home and at school where practices of socialization aim at reducing their timings to steadier rhythms. One of the implications of this way of thinking about growing up is that it allows that adults may 'uncomplete' themselves and perform themselves as participants in rapidly changing orders. For adults and for children then, time can have many speeds. An argument between adult partners is an order. It might pass into and be subsumed under a greater order such as a lasting intimate relationship. But it might build, as its consequences ramify, and bring a sudden end to the relationship. Though adults can never be children again, a partial 'becoming-child' is still available when they act through relatively few extensions. This is rather different from the flexible adulthoods of the age of uncertainty that are not based on limited extensions but on adults rapidly rebuilding themselves to fit into the ready-made orders that a new job or career segment involves. 'Becoming-child' is living in the small and temporary, but it can always form the kernel of wider more durable change.

The view of growing up that we have developed might tempt us to take a Romantic (James *et al.* 1998) view of childhood and to stereotype children once again as the embodiment of natural powers of imagination or creativity that are sadly lost to adults. But there is no need to adopt this view. Imagination and creativity are human characteristics. As such they are not the exclusive possession of children. For imagined orders to become stable and lasting however, imagination and creativity must be slowed and stilled by extension. Given this, we can consider this book part of its author's own 'becoming-adult'.

References

Alanen, L. (1994) Gender and generation: feminism and the child question, in J. Qvortrup, M. Bardy, G. Sgritta and H. Wintersberger (eds) *Childhood Matters: Social Theory, Practice and Politics*. Aldershot: Avebury.

Alderson, P. (2000) *Young Children's Rights: Exploring Beliefs, Principles and Practice*. London: Jessica Kingsley.

Ariès, P. (1962) *Centuries of Childhood*. London: Jonathan Cape.

Arthur, M.B. and Rousseau, D.M. (eds) (1996) *The Boundaryless Career: A New Employment Principle for a New Organizational Era*. New York: Oxford University Press.

Arthur, M.B., Inkson, K. and Pringle, J.K. (1999) *The New Careers: Individual Action and Economic Change*. London: Sage.

Baker, R., Panter-Brick, C. and Todd, A. (1996) Street children in Nepal, *Childhood*, 3(2): 171–93.

Bauman, Z. (1987) *Legislators and Interpreters*. Cambridge: Polity.

Beck, U. (1998) *Democracy without Enemies*. Cambridge: Polity.

Boserup, E. (1989) *Women's Role in Economic Development*. London: Earthscan.

Buckingham, D. (2000) *After the Death of Childhood: Growing Up in the Age of Electronic Media*. Cambridge: Polity.

Castells, M. (1996) *The Rise of the Network Society*. Oxford: Blackwell.

Castells, M. (1997) *The Power of Identity*. Oxford: Blackwell.

Cockburn, T. (1995) The Devil in the city: working class children in Manchester 1860–1914. Paper presented to British Sociological Association conference, University of Leicester, 11 April.

Coleman, J.S. (1961) *The Adolescent Society: The Social Life of the Teenager and its Impact on Education*. New York: Free Press of Glencoe.

Coleman, J.S. (1994) Social capital, human capital and investment in youth, in A.C. Petersen and J.T. Mortimer (eds) *Youth Unemployment and Society*. Cambridge: Cambridge University Press.

Commission of the European Communities (1995) *Teaching and Learning: Towards a Learning Society*. Luxembourg: Office for Official Publications of the European Communities.

Connolly, M. and Ennew, J. (1996) Introduction: children out of place, *Childhood*, 3(2): 131–47.

Deleuze, G. and Guattari, F. (1972) *L'Anti-Oedipe: capitalisme et schizophrénie*. Paris: Les Editions de Minuit.

Deleuze, G. and Guattari, F. (1977) *Anti-Oedipus: Capitalism and Schizophrenia*. New York: Viking.

Deleuze, G. and Guatarri, F. (1980) *Mille plateaux: capitalisme et schizophrénie*. Paris: Les Editions de Minuit.

Deleuze, G. and Guattari, F. (1988) *A Thousand Plateaus: Capitalism and Schizophrenia*. London: Athlone.

Dencik, L. (1989) Growing up in the postmodern age, *Acta Sociologica*, 32: 155–80.

Derrida, J. (1967) *De la grammatologie*. Paris: Les Editions de Minuit.

Derrida, J. (1976) *Of Grammatology*. Baltimore, Md: Johns Hopkins University Press.

Derrida, J. (1997) *Politics of Friendship*. London: Verso.

Diken, B. (1998) *Strangers, Ambivalence and Social Theory*. Aldershot: Ashgate.

Donzelot, J. (1979) *The Policing of Families*. Baltimore, Md: Johns Hopkins University Press.

Durkheim, E. (1964) *The Division of Labour in Society*. London: Macmillan.

Edwards, R. (1997) *Changing Places? Flexibility, Lifelong Learning and a Learning Society*. London: Routledge.

Elvin, L. (1977) *The Place of Commonsense in Educational Thought*. London: Allen & Unwin.

Ennew, J. (1995) Outside childhood: street children's rights, in B. Franklin (ed.) *The Handbook of Children's Rights: Comparative Policy and Practice*. London: Routledge.

Etzioni, A. (1993) *The Spirit of Community: Rights, Responsibilities and the Communitarian Agenda*. London: Fontana.

Foucault, M. (1977) *Discipline and Punish: The Birth of the Prison*. London: Allen Lane.

Friedan, B. (1963) *The Feminine Mystique*. London: Gollancz.

Fukuyama, F. (1995) *Trust: The Social Virtues and the Creation of Prosperity*. London: Hamish Hamilton.

Galbraith, J.K. (1971) *The New Industrial State*, 2nd edn. Boston, Mass.: Houghton Mifflin.

Garfinkel, H. (1967) *Studies in Ethnomethodology*. Englewood Cliffs, NJ: Prentice Hall.

Gasché, R. (1994) *Inventions of Difference: On Jacques Derrida*. Cambridge, Mass.: Harvard University Press.

General Assembly of the United Nations (1989) *UN Convention on the Rights of the Child*. www.un.org.

Giddens, A. (1992) *The Transformation of Intimacy*. Cambridge: Polity.

Glauser, B. (1997) Street children: deconstructing a construct, in A. James and A. Prout (eds) *Constructing and Reconstructing Childhood: Contemporary Issues in the Sociological Study of Childhood*, 2nd edn. London: Falmer.

Godoy, A.S. (1999) 'Our right is the right to be killed': making rights real on the streets of Guatemala City, *Childhood*, 6(4): 423–42.

Greer, G. (1971) *The Female Eunuch*. London: Palladin.

Harvey, D. (1989) *The Condition of Postmodernity*. Oxford: Blackwell.

Hegel, G.W.F. (1991) *Elements of the Philosophy of Right*. Cambridge: Cambridge University Press.

Heritage, J. (1984) *Garfinkel and Ethnomethodology*. Cambridge: Polity.

Home Office (1991) *The Criminal Justice Act 1991*. London: Her Majesty's Stationery Office.

Home Office (1998) *The Crime and Disorder Act*. London: Her Majesty's Stationery Office.

Home Office and Department of Health (1992) *Memorandum of Good Practice on Video Recorded Interviews with Child Witnesses for Criminal Proceedings*. London: Her Majesty's Stationery Office.

Hopkins, E. (1994) *Childhood Transformed: Working Class Children in Nineteenth-Century England*. Manchester: Manchester University Press.

Huston, A.C. (ed.) (1991) *Children in Poverty: Child Development and Public Policy*. Cambridge: Cambridge University Press.

Hutchby, I. and Moran-Ellis, J. (1998) *Children and Social Competence: Arenas of Action*. London: Falmer.

Illich, I. (1971) *Deschooling Society*. London: Calder.

James, A. (1996) Learning to be friends, *Childhood*, 3(3): 313–30.

James, A. and Prout, A. (eds) (1997) *Constructing and Reconstructing Childhood: Contemporary Issues in the Sociological Study of Childhood*, 2nd edn. London: Falmer.

James, A., Jenks, C. and Prout, A. (1998) *Theorizing Childhood*. Cambridge: Polity.

King, M. (1997) *A Better World for Children: Explorations in Morality and Authority*. London: Routledge.

Latour, B. (1987) *Science in Action: How to Follow Scientists and Engineers through Society*. Milton Keynes: Open University Press.

Latour, B. (1988) *The Pasteurization of France*. Cambridge, Mass.: Harvard University Press.

Law, J. (1998) *Actor Network Theory and After*. Oxford: Blackwell.

Lee, N.M. (1998a) Two speeds: how are real stabilities possible?, in R. Chia (ed.) *Organized Worlds: Explorations in Technology and Organization with Robert Cooper*. London: Routledge.

Lee, N.M. (1998b) Childhood and self-representation: the view from technology, *Anthropology in Action*, 5(3): 13–21.

Lee, N.M. (1998c) Towards an immature sociology, *The Sociological Review*, 46(3): 458–82.

Lee, N.M. (1999) The challenge of childhood: distributions of childhood's ambiguity in adult institutions, *Childhood*, 6(4): 455–74.

Lister, I. (ed.) (1974) *Deschooling: A Reader*. Cambridge: Cambridge University Press.

Livingstone, E. (1987) *Making Sense of Ethnomethodology*. London: Routledge and Kegan Paul.

Lyotard, J.F. (1984) *The Postmodern Condition*. Manchester: Manchester University Press.

McLanahan, S.S., Astone, N.M. and Marks, N.F. (1991) The role of mother only families in reproducing poverty, in A.C. Huston (ed.) *Children in Poverty: Child Development and Public Policy*. Cambridge: Cambridge University Press.

Marx, K. and Engels, F. (1970) *The German Ideology: Part 1*. London: Lawrence and Wishart.

Marx, K. and Engels, F. (1999) *The Communist Manifesto*. Boston, Mass.: Bedford.

Morrow, V. (1999) Conceptualising social capital in relation to the well-being of children and young people: a critical review, *Sociological Review*, 47(4): 744–65.

Munro, R. (1996) A consumption view of self: extension, exchange and identity, in S. Edgell, K. Hetherington and A. Warde (eds) *Consumption Matters: The Production and Experience of Consumption*. Oxford: Blackwell.

Murray, L. (1991) *Les Murray: Collected Poems*. London: Minerva.

Nuffield Foundation (1967) *I Do and I Understand*. London: W. and R. Chambers and John Murray.

Parsons, T. (1951) *The Social System*. London: Routledge and Kegan Paul.

Parsons, T. (1956) The American family: its relation to personality and the social structure, in T. Parsons and R.F. Bales (eds) *Family, Socialisation and Interaction Process*. London: Routledge and Kegan Paul.

Parsons, T. (1971) The normal American family, in B. Adams and T. Weirath (eds) *Readings on the Sociology of the Family*. Chicago: Markham.

Parton, N. (1985) *The Politics of Child Abuse*. London: Macmillan.

Pedersen, S. (1993) *Family, Dependence and the Origins of the Welfare State: Britain and France 1914–1945*. Cambridge: Cambridge University Press.

Piaget, J. (1955) *The Child's Construction of Reality*. London: Routledge and Kegan Paul.

Pickvance, C. (1999) Housing and housing policy, in J. Baldock, N. Manning, S. Miller and S. Vickerstaff (eds) *Social Policy*. Oxford: Oxford University Press.

Pigot, T., Kilkerr, A., Parker, R. *et al.* (1989) *Report of the Advisory Group on Video-Evidence*. London: Her Majesty's Stationery Office.

Plato (1994) *Republic*. Oxford: Oxford University Press.

Portes, A. and Landolt, P. (1996) The downside of social capital, *The American Prospect*, 26: 18–21.

Postman, N. (1983) *The Disappearance of Childhood*. London: W.H. Allen.

Putnam, R.D. (1993) *Making Democracy Work: Civic Traditions in Modern Italy*. Princeton, NJ: Princeton University Press.

Qvortrup, J. (1994) Childhood matters: an introduction, in J. Qvortrup, M. Bardy, G. Sgritta and H. Wintersberger (eds) *Childhood Matters: Social Theory, Practice and Politics*. Aldershot: Avebury.

Qvortrup, J. (1997) A voice for children in statistical and social accounting: a plea for children's right to be heard, in A. James and A. Prout (eds) *Constructing and Reconstructing Childhood: Contemporary Issues in the Sociological Study of Childhood*, 2nd edn. London: Falmer.

Qvortrup, J. (2000) Macroanalysis of childhood, in P. Christensen and A. James (eds) *Research with Children: Perspectives and Practices*. London: Falmer.

Risman, B.J. (1998) *Gender Vertigo: American Families in Transition*. New Haven, Conn.: Yale University Press.

Rose, N. (1989) *Governing the Soul*. London: Routledge.

Scheper-Hughes, N. and Hoffman, D. (1998) Brazilian apartheid: street kids and the struggle for urban space, in N. Scheper-Hughes and C. Sargent (eds) *Small Wars: The Cultural Politics of Childhood*. Berkeley: University of California Press.

Sennett, R. (1971) *The Uses of Disorder*. London: Penguin.

Serres, M. (1982) *Hermes: Literature, Science, Philosophy*. Baltimore, Md: Johns Hopkins University Press.

Sibley, D. (1995) Families and domestic routines: constructing the boundaries of childhood, in S. Pile and N. Thrift (eds) *Mapping the Subject: Geographies of Cultural Transformation*. London: Routledge.

Smart, C. and Neale, B. (1999) *Family Fragments?* London: Polity.

Smith, D.E. (1987) *The Everyday World as Problematic: A Feminist Sociology*. Boston, Mass.: North-Eastern University Press.

Smith, R. and Wynne, B. (eds) (1989) *Expert Evidence: Interpreting Science in the Law*. London: Routledge.

Snyder, M.C. and Tadesse, M. (1995) *African Women and Development: A History*. London: Zed.

Social Exclusion Unit (1998) *Bringing Britain Together: A National Strategy for Neighborhood Renewal*. London: Her Majesty's Stationery Office.

Somekh, B. (2000) New technology and learning: policy and practice in the UK, 1980–2010, *Education and Information Technologies*, 5(1): 19–38.

Spinoza, B. (1994) *A Spinoza Reader: The Ethics and Other Works*. Princeton, NJ: Princeton University Press.

Stainton Rogers, R. and Stainton Rogers, W. (1992) *Stories of Childhood: Shifting Agendas of Child Concern*. London: Harvester-Wheatsheaf.

Tavor Bannet, E. (1989) *Structuralism and the Logic of Dissent: Barthes, Derrida, Foucault, Lacan*. London: Macmillan.

Turner, R. (ed.) (1974) *Ethnomethodology: Selected Readings*. Harmondsworth: Penguin.

Van Beers, H. (1996) A plea for a child-centred approach in research with street children, *Childhood*, 3(2): 195–201.

Wacquant, L.J.D. (1996) The rise of advanced marginality: notes on its nature and implications, *Acta Sociologica*, 39(2): 121–39.

Wacquant, L.J.D. (1999) America as social dystopia, in P. Bourdieu (ed.) *The Weight of the World: Social Suffering in Contemporary Society*. London: Polity.

Walker Perry, N. and Wrightsman, L.S. (1991) *The Child Witness: Legal Issues and Dilemmas*. London: Sage.

Walkerdine, V. (1984) Developmental psychology and the child-centred pedagogy: the insertion of Piaget into early education, in J. Henriques, W. Hollway, C. Urwin, C. Venn and V. Walkerdine (eds) *Changing the Subject: Psychology, Social Regulation and Subjectivity*. London: Methuen.

Weber, M. (1964) *The Protestant Ethic and the Spirit of Capitalism*. London: Unwin.

Whiteford, L.M. (1998) Children's health as accumulated capital: structural adjustment in the Dominican Republic and Cuba, in N. Scheper-Hughes and C. Sargent (eds) *Small Wars: The Cultural Politics of Childhood*. Berkeley: University of California Press.

Whitehead, A.N. (1929) *Process and Reality: An Essay in Cosmology*. New York: Social Science Book Store.

Wrong, D. (1961) The over-socialized conception of man in modern sociology, *American Sociological Review*, 26: 183–93.

Index

SOCIAL EXCLUSION

David Byrne

- What does the term 'social exclusion' mean and who are the 'socially excluded'?
- Why has there been such a significant increase in 'social exclusion'?
- How can we attempt to tackle this and the problems associated with it?

'Social exclusion' is the buzz phrase for the complex range of social problems which derive from the substantial increase in social inequality in western societies. This timely and engaging volume examines these problems in societies where manufacturing industry is no longer the main basis for employment and the universal welfare states established after the Second World War are under attack. It reviews theories of social exclusion, including the Christian democratic and social democratic assertions of solidarity with which the term originated, Marxist accounts of the recreation of the reserve army of labour, and neo-liberal assertions of the sovereignty of the market in which the blame for exclusion is assigned to the excluded themselves.

Drawing on a wide variety of empirical evidence, the author concludes that the origins of social exclusion lie with the creation of a new post-industrial order founded on the exploitation of low paid workers within western capitalism, and that social policies have actually helped to create an unequal social order as opposed to simply reacting to economic forces. This controversial but accessible text will be essential reading for undergraduate courses on social exclusion within sociology, politics, economics, geography and social policy, as well as students on professional courses and practitioners in social work, community work, urban planning and management, health and housing.

Contents

176pp   0 335 19974 7 (Paperback)   0 335 19975 5 (Hardback)

CITIZENSHIP IN A GLOBAL AGE

SOCIETY, CULTURE, POLITICS

Gerard Delanty

- What is citizenship?
- Is global citizenship possible?
- Can cosmopolitanism provide an alternative to globalization?

Citizenship in a Global Age provides a comprehensive and concise overview of the main debates on citizenship and the implications of globalization. It argues that citizenship is no longer defined by nationality and the nation state, but has become de-territorialized and fragmented into the separate discourses of rights, participation, responsibility and identity. Gerard Delanty claims that cosmopolitanism is increasingly becoming a significant force in the global world due to new expressions of cultural identity, civic ties, human rights, technological innovations, ecological sustainability and political mobilization. Citizenship is no longer exclusively about the struggle for social equality but has become a major site of battles over cultural identity and demands for the recognition of group difference. Delanty argues that globalization both threatens and supports cosmopolitan citizenship. Critical of the prospects for a global civil society, he defends the alternative idea of a more limited cosmopolitan public sphere as a basis for new kinds of citizenship that have emerged in a global age.

Contents

192pp   0 335 20489 9 (Paperback)   0 335 20490 2 (Hardback)